Calisthenic Beginners: Transform Your Body.

"Learn to perform simple free-body exercises at home, gain muscle mass and lose weight easily!"

By Francesco Martini

Copyright © 2024 by Francesco Martini

All rights reserved.

No part of this book may be reproduced in any form without the written permission of the publisher or author, except as permitted by American copyright law

Chapter 1: Introduction to Calisthenics 7
1.1 What is Calisthenics? Definition and brief history 7
1.2 Benefits of Calisthenics: Strength, Flexibility and Endurance 8
1.3 Why choose Calisthenics? Advantages over other types of training 10
1.4 What to expect from this book 12
1.5 How to prepare mentally and physically to get started 14

Chapter 2: Fundamental Principles of Calisthenics 16
2.1 Understanding of basic form and technique 16
2.2 Importance of heating and cooling 18
2.3 How to avoid common injuries 20
2.4 Setting short- and long-term goals 22
2.5 Building a basic training routine 23

Chapter 3: Basic Exercises 27
3.1 Overview of fundamental exercises 27
3.2 Push-ups and variations 30
3.3 Pull-ups and variations 33
3.4 Squats and variations 37
3.5 Plank and variations 40

Chapter 4: Progressions and Increasing Difficulty 44
4.1 Introduction to progressions 44
4.2 Modify exercises to increase intensity 46

4.3 Using your own body weight to increase the challenge 48

4.4 Advanced exercises and their benefits 50

4.5 Monitoring progress and adjusting training.......... 53

Chapter 5: Workouts and Type Programs 56

5.1 Create a weekly training program............................ 56

5.2 Examples of daily routines 58

5.3 Variations to prevent monotony................................ 65

5.4 Adapt training to your needs..................................... 67

5.5 Tips for staying consistent 69

Chapter 6: Nutrition for Calisthenics 72

6.1 Fundamentals of nutrition for fitness 72

6.2 Foods to prefer and avoid 74

6.3 Meal planning to optimize performance 76

6.4 Supplements: use and advice.................................... 79

6.5 Maintaining a food diary.. 81

Chapter 7: Weight Management and Body Composition 85

7.1 Relationship between Calisthenics and weight loss 85

7.2 Methods for measuring body composition 88

7.3 Strategies for losing weight and gaining muscle.. 91

7.4 Analysis and studies of some cases........................ 93

7.5 Achieving and maintaining ideal weight................ 96

Chapter 8: Advanced Breathing and Concentration Techniques in Calisthenics 100

8.1 Breathing Techniques to Improve Performance 100

8.2 Using Meditation to Improve Concentration 103

8.3 Visualization Techniques for Mental Preparation 106

8.4 Impact of Breathing on Post-Workout Recovery 108

8.5 Integrating Breathing and Meditation into the Daily Routine 111

Chapter 9: Overcoming Obstacles 114

9.1 Identifying and overcoming mental barriers 114

9.2 Managing muscle fatigue and pain 117

9.3 Tips for recovery and recuperation 120

9.4 Maintaining long-term motivation 123

9.5 How to handle plateaus 126

Chapter 10: Going Beyond the Beginner 130

10.1 When you are ready for the intermediate level ... 130

10.2 Introduction to more complex exercises 133

10.3 Creating a community of support 139

10.4 Continuing learning and growth 142

10.5 Planning for the future of your fitness journey .. 145

A GIFT FOR YOU!

Dear Reader,

Thank you for choosing to purchase [name of book]! To express my gratitude, I have decided to offer you an exclusive gift:

THE 30-DAY SIX PACK CHALLENGE

Through this ebook, you will discover: In my book you will find a personalized program to shape the abdomen in 30 days, suitable for all levels. It is simple, effective and designed to deliver real results. If you've tried everything without success, this is the method you've been waiting for: the perfect gift to achieve your goals!

To access your free and exclusive gift, simply scan the following QR code:

I hope this gift adds further value to your reading experience and helps you achieve your goals. Happy reading and thanks again for your support!

Chapter 1: Introduction to Calisthenics

1.1 What is Calisthenics? Definition and brief history

Calisthenics is a form of physical training that emphasizes the use of body weight to improve strength, flexibility and agility. Unlike workouts that require the use of heavy equipment or machines, calisthenics uses primarily free-body exercises, making it accessible to anyone, anywhere. This form of exercise includes a variety of rhythmic movements that often involve jumping, bending, pulling, and pushing. Common exercises include push-ups, pull-ups, squats, and sit-ups, which can be modulated in intensity and difficulty to suit various fitness levels.

Historically, calisthenics has deep roots dating back to ancient Greece. The term comes from the Greek words "kallos," meaning beauty, and "sthenos," meaning strength. The ancient Greeks practiced it not only to improve physical strength, but also to develop elegance and grace in their movements, components considered essential in the preparation of their warriors and athletes. Over the centuries, this practice has evolved and spread in various forms, including military and school gymnastic exercises in Europe and the United States, until it has become a key component of modern training.

In the 20th century, calisthenics has seen renewed interest because of its effectiveness and simplicity. It has become an integral part of military and athlete physical training, as well as popular in schools as a means of promoting physical activity among young people. More recently, the street workout movement has transformed calisthenics into a sport in its own right, with competitions and demonstrations attracting participants from around the world.

Calisthenics is not only an effective training method, it is also a philosophy of life for many. Because it is easily scaled from simple to complex movements, it allows individuals of any fitness level to begin a journey toward physical well-being.

Moving on to 1.2, we will see how calisthenics, through the use of fundamental exercises, can greatly improve not only muscle strength but also flexibility and endurance. These benefits are essential not only for overall physical health but also for improved performance in a variety of daily and sports activities. By increasing strength, flexibility, and endurance, calisthenics becomes a powerful tool for transforming the body, improving health, and increasing quality of life.

1.2 Benefits of Calisthenics: Strength, Flexibility and Endurance

Calisthenics, known for its simplicity and effectiveness, offers a wide range of benefits that make it an ideal choice for anyone wishing to improve their fitness. Among the main benefits, calisthenics increases muscle strength, flexibility, and endurance. Let's explore how these aspects translate into tangible benefits for health and physical well-being.

Strength: One of the main goals of calisthenics is to build muscle strength. Using body weight as resistance, calisthenics exercises stimulate muscles to develop and become stronger. Movements such as pull-ups, push-ups, and squats are not only effective for working specific muscle groups, but also engage multiple muscles at once, thus improving overall body strength. This type of training promotes muscle hypertrophy, tendon strengthening and joint stabilization, which are essential for a well-balanced and functional body.

Flexibility: Often overlooked in traditional strength training, flexibility is crucial for a wide range of motion and for preventing injury. Calisthenics naturally incorporates exercises that improve flexibility, such as dynamic and static stretching integrated into routines. Movements that require a wide range of motion, such as bridge or L-sit, extend joint range of motion and improve muscle elasticity. The flexibility gained through calisthenics also helps improve posture and reduce the risk of injury during other physical activities.

Endurance: Physical endurance is another key pillar of calisthenics. Workouts are often structured in circuits or sets that keep the heart rate high, combining cardiovascular conditioning with muscle strengthening. This type of training not only increases muscular endurance, but also improves cardiovascular capacity, allowing exercise to be performed for longer periods without fatigue. In addition, the endurance built through calisthenics improves performance in a variety of sports and daily activities, making it easier to manage physical and mental stress.

In the next section, 1.3, we will further explore why calisthenics is a preferred choice over other training methods. We will explore the specific advantages that make it ideal not only for improving fitness, but also for easily integrating into daily life, offering practical and flexible solutions for anyone wishing to begin a sustainable fitness journey without the need for expensive investments in equipment or subscriptions.

1.3 Why choose Calisthenics? Advantages over other types of training

Calisthenics stands out as an extremely effective and accessible form of exercise, offering numerous advantages over other types of workouts. These benefits make calisthenics an ideal option for anyone, regardless of fitness level or available resources.

Cost-efficiency: One of the greatest advantages of calisthenics is its cost-efficiency. Unlike other forms of training that require expensive equipment, gym memberships or the purchase of weights and machines, calisthenics relies solely on body weight. This makes it a practical and cost-effective way to maintain fitness without having to invest in equipment.

Versatility and convenience: Calisthenics can be practiced anywhere, whether inside a room at home, in a park, or in confined spaces, eliminating the need to travel to a specific gym. This versatility makes it especially suitable for those with busy lifestyles or those who travel frequently, allowing them to maintain a consistent workout routine without interruption.

Adaptability: Unlike other training regimens that may require a certain level of experience or skill, calisthenics is highly adaptable and can be modulated to meet the needs of any individual, regardless of their initial physical condition. This makes calisthenics extremely inclusive, offering everyone from beginners to advanced athletes the opportunity to improve their fitness in a progressive and safe manner.

Holistic body development: Calisthenics promotes harmonious and proportionate physical development because the exercises stress multiple muscle groups simultaneously. This contrasts with workouts that focus on specific machines, which often isolate individual muscles, limiting the muscle synergy needed for complex, natural movements.

Improved mind-body connection: Calisthenics exercises require considerable concentration to maintain proper form and control various muscle groups simultaneously. This not only improves physical strength but also body awareness, increasing the mind-body connection. This aspect is less pronounced in forms of training that use guided machinery, where the movement is often more mechanical and less cognitively engaging.

Long-term benefits: Practicing calisthenics regularly not only increases strength, flexibility and endurance but also promotes long-term health. It reduces the risk of musculoskeletal injuries by improving posture and muscle control and contributes to better cardiovascular health.

Moving on to the next point, 1.4, "What to Expect from this Book," we will elaborate on how these benefits are accessible through a step-by-step guide that maximizes the potential of calisthenics. The book will not only provide detailed instructions for performing various exercises, but will also offer practical tips for integrating the workout into daily life, ensuring that each reader can achieve his or her fitness goals effectively and sustainably.

1.4 What to expect from this book

This book is designed as a comprehensive guide for anyone who wants to explore calisthenics, a form of exercise based on the use of body weight. Through reading it, readers can expect to receive all the information and resources they need to begin and progress in their fitness journey with calisthenics, regardless of their starting level.

Complete Exercise Guide: This book provides detailed instruction on a wide range of calisthenics exercises, from the most basic to the most advanced. Each exercise is clearly described, including the steps involved, the muscles involved, and tips for avoiding common mistakes. Illustrations accompany the texts to ensure that each movement is easily understood and correctly performed.

Customizable workout programs: A variety of workout programs will be presented, designed to suit various fitness levels and personal goals. These programs are structured to guide readers through logical progressions, increasing the intensity and complexity of exercises as strength and confidence are gained.

Nutrition Advice: Understanding the importance of nutrition in supporting a calisthenics regimen is essential for optimal results. This book offers practical advice on how to balance diet to promote muscle recovery, strength gains, and weight loss. Examples of diet plans that complement physical efforts will also be provided.

Strategies for tracking progress: Maintaining motivation can be difficult, especially in the beginning. Therefore, this book introduces effective methods for tracking improvements, both in physical performance and overall well-being. These tools help you visualize progress, set new goals, and adjust workouts based on your body's responses.

Motivation Support: Techniques for overcoming mental obstacles, increasing consistency and staying motivated will be explored. The book aims to build a long-term relationship with calisthenics by providing tips for keeping training challenging and rewarding.

Testimonials and Case Studies: To inspire readers and demonstrate the versatility of calisthenics, the book includes stories of individuals who have transformed their bodies and lives through this practice. These narratives offer real, tangible perspectives on the benefits of calisthenics and how it can be adapted to different needs and lifestyles.

Continuing with Section 1.5, "How to Prepare Mentally and Physically to Get Started," the book will guide readers through the initial preparations needed to tackle a new fitness regimen. This section will emphasize the importance of proper mindset and physical preparation, ensuring that readers are fully equipped to embark on their calisthenics journey with confidence and enthusiasm. The focus will be on how to set up an environment conducive to training and how to mentally approach a new challenge, establishing the foundation for a successful fitness journey.

1.5 How to prepare mentally and physically to get started

Embarking on a new fitness journey such as calisthenics requires proper preparation on both the mental and physical levels. This section of the book provides effective strategies to ensure that readers are ready to begin their workout as safely and productively as possible.

Mental Preparation:

1. **Set realistic goals**: Before starting, it is crucial to clearly define what you want to achieve with calisthenics. Goals should be specific, measurable, attainable, relevant and timed (SMART). Whether it is to increase strength, improve flexibility, lose weight, or simply maintain an active lifestyle, having clear goals can serve as motivation and guidance.

2. **Develop a positive mindset**: The attitude with which you approach your new training regimen can make the difference between success and failure. Encouraging yourself with positive thoughts and visualizing success can help you overcome initial challenges.

3. **Accepting your limits**: It is important to recognize and accept your current limits to avoid frustration and injury. Progress in calisthenics happens gradually, and accepting that there will be better days than others is critical to steady growth.

Physical Preparation:

1. **Health assessment**: Before beginning any exercise program, it is advisable to have an assessment of your health. A medical check-up can reveal any conditions that might limit physical activity and suggest specific adaptations needed for one's well-being.

2. **Create a suitable space**: Preparing a comfortable and safe training area is essential. This space does not have to be large, but it should be free of obstacles and hazards. A yoga mat, enough space to move freely, and good ventilation can make a big difference.

3. **Proper clothing and equipment**: Although calisthenics requires little equipment, wearing the right clothing can enhance the workout experience. Comfortable clothes that do not restrict movement and shoes with good support are recommended to make it easier to perform the exercises and prevent injuries.

4. **Warm-up**: Starting every training session with a proper warm-up is vital. Warming up increases body temperature, improves muscle elasticity, and reduces the risk of injury. Warm-up exercises can include jogging in place, light jumping jacks, or dynamic movements that mimic calisthenics exercises.

Preparing properly both mentally and physically is the crucial first step in the journey to wellness with calisthenics. With clear goals, a positive mindset, an appropriate environment and good initial fitness, readers will be ready to take the first confident steps toward improving their fitness. The next section, 2.1 "Understanding Basic Form and Technique," will delve into how to properly perform calisthenics exercises to maximize the benefits and minimize the risk of injury, thus building a solid foundation on which to build the rest of the training program.

Chapter 2: Fundamental Principles of Calisthenics

2.1 Understanding of basic form and technique

Success in calisthenics is highly dependent on proper exercise execution, which not only optimizes results but also prevents injury. This section of the book is devoted to exploring in detail the importance of proper form and technique when performing calisthenics exercises.

Fundamentals of proper form: Good form is not only essential for safety, but also to ensure that each exercise is as effective as possible. For example, in push-ups, maintaining a straight line from neck to toe without letting the hips sag or rise too much can prevent stress on the back and shoulders and focus the effectiveness of the exercise on the pectoral and arm muscles.

Body alignment and balance: Every calisthenics exercise requires precise body alignment to maximize effectiveness and minimize the risk of injury. Proper alignment involves activation of the right muscles and balanced distribution of body weight. For example, during squats, the feet should be shoulder-width apart with the toes pointing slightly outward, and body weight should be evenly distributed on the heels and not the toes.

Control and stability: Control in movement is vital, especially when performing exercises that involve lifting or balancing. For example, during bar pulls, it is important to pull yourself up in a controlled movement, avoiding rocking or using momentum, to ensure that the muscles in the arms and back are effectively stimulated.

Proper breathing: Breathing plays a crucial role in performance and endurance during exercise. Teaching readers to breathe correctly through exercise-inhaling and exhaling at specific times-can significantly increase their ability to perform exercises more intensely and for longer periods. For example, exhaling during the most challenging part of an exercise and inhaling during relaxation can help maintain the pace and effectiveness of the workout.

Practice and repetition: As with any skill, mastery of form and technique requires practice and repetition. It is essential to encourage readers not to rush progress, but to focus on quality of movement rather than quantity. Consistent practice with a focus on proper form will ensure that movements become second nature, reducing the risk of injury and increasing the effectiveness of training.

These fundamental concepts of form and technique in calisthenics not only prepare practitioners to perform exercises safely and effectively but also establish the foundation for the next discussion point, 2.2 "Importance of warm-up and cool-down." Adopting proper technique complements the practice of good warm-up and cool-down routines, which further enhance performance and reduce the risk of injury, thus completing a holistic approach to training.

2.2 Importance of heating and cooling

Warm-up and cool-down are essential components of any training regimen, but they are often underestimated or skipped by many fitness practitioners. This section examines why these practices are crucial in calisthenics, not only to improve performance and training effectiveness, but also to prevent injury, linking to Section 2.3 below, "How to Avoid Common Injuries."

Warm-up: Preparing the Body for Exercise

Warming up serves to prepare the body and mind for upcoming physical activity. It is especially important in calisthenics, where exercises require extensive use of body weight and often involve complex and intense movements.

1. **Increased body temperature**: A good warm-up gradually increases body temperature, making muscles more elastic and less susceptible to tearing or stretching. This is critical for exercises such as squats, pull-ups and push-ups, which put considerable strain on the muscles.

2. **Improved blood circulation**: Activating circulation through warm-up exercises ensures that more oxygen and nutrients reach the muscles, which is vital for performance and endurance.

3. **Psychological preparation**: The warm-up also helps focus the mind on the upcoming training session,

improving concentration and preparing psychologically to engage in the exercises.

An effective warm-up can include light jogging, jumping jacks, joint mobility exercises and dynamic stretching, all geared toward preparing the body for more intense movements.

Cooling: Facilitating Post-Workout Recovery

After an intense calisthenics session, cooling down helps the body gradually return to a state of rest, a process just as important as warming up.

1. **Reducing heart rate**: Cooling exercises such as walking or light stretching help to gradually reduce heart rate and stabilize blood pressure, preventing dizziness or sickness that can occur if you abruptly stop physical activity.

2. **Elimination of waste products**: Cooling helps the body eliminate waste products from muscle metabolism, such as lactic acid, which can build up during intense exercise and contribute to muscle soreness.

3. **Muscle pain prevention**: Incorporating static stretching into cooling can reduce muscle stiffness and minimize post-workout pain, improving flexibility and aiding in long-term injury prevention.

Linking with Injury Prevention

Implementing proper warm-up and cool-down routines prepares the body not only for the day's training but also for future sessions, reducing the risk of muscle and joint injuries.

This direct link to injury prevention will be further explored in the next section, 2.3 "How to Avoid Common Injuries," where we will discuss how proper warm-up and cool-down practice can be integrated into an overall fitness regimen to ensure a safe and sustained practice of calisthenics.

2.3 How to avoid common injuries

Injury prevention is a key aspect of any training program, especially in calisthenics, where the use of body weight and the complexity of movements can increase the risk of injury if not performed correctly. This section of the book offers essential strategies for reducing the risk of common injuries in calisthenics, linking to Section 2.4 below, "Setting short- and long-term goals," where the importance of safety will be integrated into training planning.

Knowledge of and respect for one's limits: First of all, it is crucial for each practitioner to know and respect his or her physical limits. This includes understanding when it is time to push harder and when it is necessary to take a break. Ignoring the body's signals can lead to injuries such as muscle tears or joint problems.

Improve technique before increasing intensity: A common mistake is trying to perform advanced movements without having mastered basic techniques first. This can lead to improper form, which is a major cause of injury in calisthenics. It is essential to spend time practicing the basic exercises and only when these are fully controlled, proceed with more challenging variations.

Use of support equipment when needed: Using support equipment, such as elastic bands or padded mats, can reduce the risk of injury. These tools can help stabilize the body while performing exercises, providing additional support that can be especially useful for beginners or while learning new movements.

Incorporating stabilization exercises and core training: A strong core (core) is essential for maintaining good posture and reducing the load on the back and joints during calisthenics exercises. Exercises such as planks, dead bugs or Russian twists strengthen the core muscles, improving overall stability and reducing the risk of injury.

Regular stretching and mobility: Including regular stretching sessions and working on mobility can greatly reduce the risk of injury. Stretching helps maintain or increase flexibility, which is vital for performing a wide range of movements in calisthenics without stressing muscles and joints.

Listen to the body and rest properly: Rest is as important as training. Recovery allows the body to repair muscle tissue and strengthen itself. Ignoring the need for rest and continuing to train even when tired or sore can easily lead to injury.

By incorporating these practices into their calisthenics regimen, practitioners can significantly reduce the risk of injury and enjoy a safe and productive fitness journey. Continuing with Section 2.4, "Setting Short- and Long-Term Goals," we will see how proper planning and setting realistic goals can not only prevent injury but also ensure consistent and satisfactory progress over time, creating a virtuous cycle of continuous improvement and safety.

2.4 Setting short- and long-term goals

Setting well-defined goals is crucial to success in any training program, including calisthenics practice. This chapter explores how to set effective short- and long-term goals that not only motivate and guide practitioners, but also help measure progress and maintain confidence during workouts. This goal setting serves as a key introduction to the next section, 2.5 "Building a Basic Workout Routine," where the goals you set will guide you to creating a personalized workout plan.

Setting SMART Goals: SMART goals are Specific, Measurable, Actionable, Relevant, and Temporally Defined. In the context of calisthenics, this might mean setting a goal to perform a certain number of consecutive pull-ups or push-ups within a specified period, or improving one's flexibility to perform a specific movement without assistance.

1. **Specific**: Goals should be clear and precise. For example, instead of "improve strength," a specific goal could be "perform 10 consecutive pull-ups."

2. **Measurable**: It is essential that you can measure your progress. If your goal is to improve flexibility, consider using a specific test to assess this periodically.

3. **Actionable**: Goals must be realistic and achievable within your current fitness level and life circumstances.

4. **Relevant**: Goals should be relevant to your personal desires and why you practice calisthenics, whether they are related to health, fitness, or specific performance.

5. **Temporally defined**: Establishing a timeline helps maintain motivation. A short-term goal might be set for the next 6 weeks, while a long-term goal might extend to 6 months or more.

Short-Term Goals: Short-term goals serve as milestones that help you stay motivated and track progress. They might include technical improvements, such as perfecting form in a specific exercise, or quantitative increases, such as increasing the number of sets and repetitions of an exercise.

Long-Term Goals: These goals are more ambitious and require a sustained commitment. They might relate to achieving an advanced level in certain exercises, such as doing a planche or performing a muscle-up, or they might target overall physical transformations, such as significant weight loss or gains in muscle mass.

Review and Adaptation of Goals: Being flexible and ready to modify goals is important. Periodic reviews allow goals to be adapted to new circumstances or progress, ensuring that they remain relevant and motivating.

The goal-setting process not only provides a clear direction for your calisthenics journey but also sets the stage for building a tailored training regimen, which will be explored in more detail in the next section, 2.5 "Building a Basic Training Routine." Here, defined goals will guide the choice of exercises and the structuring of training sessions, integrating all aspects learned so far to create a holistic and personalized plan.

2.5 Building a basic training routine

A well-structured basic training routine is the foundation for anyone beginning calisthenics. It should be designed to gradually build strength, endurance and flexibility while maintaining interest and motivation. This chapter will guide readers through the steps to create an effective routine that will be the basis for all the more advanced exercises covered in the next section, 3.1 "Overview of Fundamental Exercises."

Initial Assessment: Before beginning, it is essential to assess your current fitness level. This may include the ability to perform basic exercises such as push-ups, squats, and planks. Understanding your starting level helps you tailor your routine to avoid overloading and minimize the risk of injury.

Incorporating Variety: A basic workout routine should include a variety of exercises that work on different muscle groups for a balanced workout.

Here are some examples:

- **Strength**: Exercises such as push-ups, pull-ups, and dips to build upper body strength.
- **Core**: Exercises such as planks, crunches, and leg raises to strengthen the core.
- **Lower**: Squats, lunges, and calf raises for leg and gluteal muscles.
- **Flexibility and mobility**: Dynamic stretching and yoga can be integrated to improve flexibility and overall mobility.

Session Structure: Each training session should follow a clear and consistent structure:

1. **Warm-up**: 5-10 minutes of light warm-up to increase heart rate and prepare muscles and joints for physical activity.

2. **Main part**: 20-40 minutes of calisthenics exercises, alternating muscle groups to allow adequate rest between exercises.

3. **Cool down**: 5-10 minutes of stretching to help muscles recover and prevent post-workout muscle soreness.

Progression and Adaptability: Routines should allow realistic progressions. Exercises can be made more difficult by increasing the number of repetitions, adding more complex variations, or reducing the rest time between sets. It is important to listen to your body and adapt the intensity of the workout to prevent overload and maintain the long-term sustainability of the routine.

Frequency of Workouts: For beginners, it is recommended to start with 2-3 sessions per week, allowing interspersed rest days for recovery. As strength and endurance improve, you can gradually increase the frequency and intensity of workouts.

Documentation and Review: Keeping track of training sessions, exercises performed, repetitions and sensations can help monitor progress and identify areas that need further improvement. Reviewing routines periodically is essential to adapt them to updated physical developments and goals.

By creating a solid basic training routine, readers will have the foundation needed to progress to more complex and challenging exercises, such as those discussed in 3.1 "Overview of Fundamental Exercises" below. This natural progression ensures that practitioners develop the skills and confidence needed to explore the full potential of calisthenics.

Chapter 3: Basic Exercises

3.1 Overview of fundamental exercises

In this chapter, we will explore the basic calisthenics exercises that form the core of every effective routine. These exercises have been selected for their ability to build a solid foundation of strength, endurance and flexibility, which are essential for every practitioner from beginner to advanced. Understanding and mastering these exercises is crucial before moving on to their more complex variations, discussed in the next section, 3.2 "Push-ups and Variations."

Push-ups: Push-ups are a key exercise in calisthenics to develop upper body strength, particularly pecs, shoulders and triceps. In addition to these muscle groups, push-ups also work the core muscles, providing an overall body workout.

Pull-ups: This exercise is essential for strengthening the upper body, particularly the back, biceps and forearm muscles. Pull-ups are known for their difficulty, but they are incredibly effective for building functional strength and improving grip.

Squats: Squats are vital for developing leg and gluteal strength and stability. As a compound exercise, they also engage the core and improve mobility in the ankles and knees, which are essential for good posture and preventing injury.

Planks: Planks are one of the most effective exercises for building stability and strength in the core. This static exercise, when performed correctly, activates a wide range of stabilizing muscles throughout the body, improving posture and supporting overall function.

Dips: Focused primarily on the triceps, dips are also excellent for working the shoulders and chest. This exercise can be performed on parallel bars or on a bench for easier variations, making it accessible to beginners and advanced exercisers.

Each exercise in this overview can be adapted to increase or decrease intensity, allowing practitioners of different fitness levels to find the right challenge for their workout. It is important that each exercise is performed with the correct form to maximize the benefits and minimize the risk of injury.

Video tutorials or support from a coach can be helpful for beginners to make sure the technique is correct.

The transition from understanding and mastering these core exercises to exploring their variations offers a natural progression in calisthenics training. For example, once standard push-ups become manageable, practitioners can explore variations that further challenge strength and stability. In the next section, 3.2 "Push-ups and Variations," we will discuss how to vary this exercise to keep the workout challenging and continue to build strength and endurance in new and challenging ways.

3.2 Push-ups and variations

Push-ups are among the most versatile and fundamental exercises in calisthenics. This exercise not only strengthens the upper body, but also improves core stability and coordination. In this chapter, we will explore several variations of push-ups that can be incorporated into your routine to further challenge and stimulate your muscles in different ways, setting the stage for the next section, 3.3 "Pull-ups and Variations."

Standard Push-up: Before exploring variations, it is crucial to master the form of the standard push-up. The starting position is with hands spread shoulder-width apart, the

Straight body from head to toe, and feet together. When you lower yourself, your body should remain in a straight line, and your elbows should bend outward. It is important to keep the core contracted to support the spine and reduce the risk of back injury.

Wide-Hand Push-up: By increasing the distance between the hands well beyond shoulder width, this variation places more emphasis on the pectorals and a little less on the triceps and shoulders. It is a good option for those who wish to focus more on the outside of the pecs.

Diamond Push-up: By placing the hands close together so that the thumbs and index fingers form a "diamond" under the chest, this variation increases the intensity of the exercise on the triceps and inner chest. This type of push-up is especially useful for those who want to develop triceps strength.

One-arm push-up: This is an advanced exercise that not only challenges strength but also core balance and stability.

Performing a push-up using only one arm at a time doubles the load on that arm, significantly intensifying the exercise. It is critical to gradually build up to this variation to avoid injury.

Declined **Push-ups**: By placing the feet on an elevated surface, declined push-ups increase the intensity on the upper pectoral area and shoulders. This variation can be an effective preparation for more complex movements such as muscle-ups.

Incline Push-ups: With hands on an elevated surface and feet on the ground, incline push-ups reduce the intensity of the exercise, which is ideal for beginners or those recovering from injury. This variation helps build the strength needed to perform standard push-ups with less risk.

These push-up variations not only add diversity and challenge to your workout routine, but also allow for a logical progression that helps you build strength in a balanced and safe manner. By incorporating these variations into your program, you can steadily improve your skills in calisthenics.

Continuing with the next point, 3.3 "Pull-ups and Variations," we will explore how exercises involving pulling can complement those involving pushing, such as push-ups, for a balanced and complete overall workout. This holistic approach is essential for harmonious development and prevention of muscle imbalances.

3.3 Pull-ups and variations

Pull-ups are a fundamental exercise in calisthenics that primarily targets the back muscles but also involves biceps, forearms and shoulders. This exercise is known for its ability to build impressive upper body strength and improve grip. In this chapter, we will explore several variations of pull-ups that can help practitioners further develop their strength and endurance, creating a bridge to the next section, 3.4 "Squats and Variations," where similar techniques for the lower body will be covered.

Standard Pull-up: The standard pull-up is performed with a pronation grip (palms facing outward) slightly wider than shoulder width. This variation targets primarily the latissimus dorsi (the largest muscles in the back), with significant activation of the biceps and shoulders. Keeping the body straight and using controlled upward and downward movement is essential to maximize effectiveness and minimize the risk of injury.

Chin-ups: Chin-ups use a supination grip (palms facing inward), which places more emphasis on the biceps while still involving the back muscles. This variation is often considered slightly easier than standard pull-ups because of the greater participation of the biceps, which can help with the pulling movement.

Neutral Grip Pull-ups: Neutral grip pull-ups are performed with the hands facing each other. This grip is particularly useful for reducing stress on the shoulders, making the exercise a good option for those with joint problems or looking for a less demanding variation on the shoulders.

Wide Pull-ups: By increasing the distance between the hands well beyond shoulder width, wide pull-ups aim to intensify the work on the latissimus dorsi, increasing the difficulty of the exercise. This variation is excellent for developing back width.

Pull-ups with One Hand: This is an advanced variation that requires significant strength and grip. One-handed pull-ups not only challenge strength but also balance and coordination. It is vital to approach this variation only after gaining significant strength and technique with the other forms of pull-ups.

L-sit Pull-ups: Combining a pull-up with the L-sit position, this variation not only works the back and biceps intensely but also the core muscles. Keeping the legs elevated in a horizontal position while performing the pull-up significantly increases the difficulty of the exercise.

Incorporating these variations into your calisthenics regimen can lead to significant improvements in upper body strength and overall function. As you develop greater strength and confidence with pull-ups, you can explore these variations to keep your routine challenging and progressive.

Moving on to the next item, 3.4 "Squats and Variations," we will examine how similar exercises can be applied to develop lower body strength and endurance, ensuring a balanced and complete workout. This holistic approach is critical to building a harmonious physique and preventing muscle imbalances that could lead to injury.

3.4 Squats and variations

The squat is a fundamental exercise in calisthenics and fitness in general, known for its effectiveness in building strength, power and stability in the lower body. It primarily targets the quads, glutes and hamstrings, but when performed correctly, the squat can also engage the core and improve overall mobility. In this chapter, we will explore several squat variations that can help diversify training, introducing how these variations can be integrated before moving on to the next point, 3.5 "Planks and Variations."

Free-Body Squat: The starting point for most calisthenics practitioners is the free-body squat. This basic version is performed with the feet shoulder-width apart or slightly wider, with the toes pointing slightly outward. As you lower your body, your hips and knees bend while your glutes push back, always keeping your back straight and chest lifted. It is important to descend until the thighs are parallel to the ground, ensuring that the knees do not go past the toes.

Sumo Squat: This variation requires a wider stance with the feet further apart than shoulder width and toes pointing even more outward. The sumo squat puts more emphasis on the inner thigh muscles, glutes and even the smaller core muscles, thus improving stability.

Squat with Jump: To add an element of power and cardio, the squat with jump introduces an explosive upward jump at the end of the squat movement. This variation not only increases heart rate but also helps build explosive power in the legs, which is useful for other exercises and sports activities.

One-Leg Squat (Pistol Squat): The pistol squat is an advanced variation that requires considerable strength, balance and mobility. This squat is performed on one leg only, with the other extended in front of the body for the duration of the exercise. The pistol squat is extremely effective for developing unilateral strength and balance, as well as isolating and working intensely on each leg.

Bulgarian Squat: This type of squat is performed with one foot placed on a raised surface behind you (such as a bench or step). The Bulgarian squat increases quadriceps and gluteal isolation of the supporting leg, while also providing a significant test for stability and balance.

Integrating these squat variations into your workout routine not only adds diversity but also helps to overcome stalled phases of training by stimulating your muscles in new and challenging ways. Each variation can be adapted to increase or decrease difficulty, making squats accessible and beneficial for practitioners of all levels.

The next chapter, 3.5 "Planks and Variations," will explore how stabilizing exercises such as planks can complement squats to develop overall body strength, highlighting the importance of a balanced workout involving both the upper and lower body.

3.5 Plank and variations

The plank is an essential exercise in calisthenics, known for its effectiveness in strengthening the core, which includes the abdominal muscles, lower back muscles, and those around the hips and pelvis. Strong core muscles not only improve overall posture and stability but are also crucial for increasing performance in all other calisthenics exercises. In this chapter, we will explore several variations of the plank that can be integrated to diversify the workout routine, setting the stage for the next section, 4.1 "Introduction to Progressions."

Standard Plank: The standard plank is performed by resting the forearms on the ground with the elbows placed under the shoulders and the feet together. The body should form a straight line from head to toe, avoiding raising or lowering the hips. This position should be maintained by keeping the core muscles strongly contracted throughout the exercise.

Lateral Plank: The lateral plank targets the oblique muscles more specifically, as well as engaging the entire core. To perform a lateral plank, lean on one elbow, with your body turned to the side and legs extended. The body should form a straight line from head to toe, with the other arm positioned along the body or extended toward the ceiling for added balance.

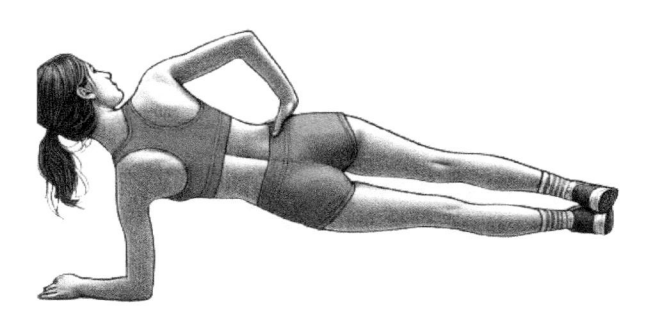

Plank with Leg Lift: From a standard plank position, alternately lift each leg off the ground. This variation increases the core challenge and also engages the glutes and lower back muscles. Be sure to keep your hips stable and do not let them fall sideways during the leg lift.

Plank with Shoulder Touch: Starting from the plank position on hands instead of elbows, raise one hand to touch the opposite shoulder, alternating between right and left. This variation not only challenges core strength but also increases the difficulty in maintaining body stability by further engaging the stabilizing muscles.

Plank Superman: The plank superman is a calisthenics exercise that combines the plank position with the superman movement. Starting from the plank position on your hands and feet, you alternately lift one arm and the opposite leg, extending them fully. This exercise strengthens the core, shoulders and back.

Integrating these plank variations into a workout routine helps not only to strengthen the core but also to prevent monotony, keeping the workout challenging and engaging. Each variation can be adapted to increase or decrease difficulty, making the plank a versatile exercise suitable for all fitness levels.

In the next chapter, 4.1 "Introduction to Progressions," we will explore how these variations can be structured into a systematic progression, allowing practitioners to continue to develop their strength and skill in calisthenics, ensuring consistent and measurable growth over time. This methodical approach is critical to building not only physical ability but also confidence in each exercise performed.

Chapter 4: Progressions and Increasing Difficulty

4.1 Introduction to progressions

Progressions in calisthenics are the gradual process of moving from simpler to more complex movements to improve strength, endurance, flexibility and body control. This progressive practice allows anyone, regardless of starting level, to develop advanced skills over time. This chapter introduces the basic principles of progressions, linking to the next section 4.2, "Modifying Exercises to Increase Intensity," in which we will explore specific strategies for making exercises more challenging.

Concept of Progression: Progression is a key concept in calisthenics. Each exercise can be adapted to increase or decrease in difficulty, allowing practitioners to gradually progress to more complex variations. The goal of progressions is to keep the workout challenging enough to promote muscle growth and skill, without overloading the body.

Identifying Starting Level: Before beginning a progression, it is essential to honestly assess one's current capabilities. This helps you identify a realistic starting point and develop a set of progressive goals that can be achieved safely. An assessment might include how many repetitions you can perform of a specific exercise or how long you can maintain a plank.

Elements of Effective Progression:

1. **Gradual Increments**: Increases in difficulty should be small and measurable, such as increasing the number of repetitions, reducing the rest time between sets, or adding more challenging variations.

2. **Rest and Recovery**: Progressions should always include adequate rest periods to allow muscles to recover and adapt to the new intensity. Excessive fatigue can slow progress and increase the risk of injury.

3. **Feedback and Monitoring**: Keeping track of progress and listening to the body's signals is essential to identify when it is time to advance to the next stage of progression.

Examples of Progression:

- **Push-ups**: Starting with prone push-ups, you can gradually move to free-body push-ups, then to variations such as diamond push-ups and finally to one-arm push-ups.

- **Pull-ups**: Start with assisted pull-ups (with rubber bands or support), then move to standard pull-ups, followed by wide pull-ups and finally muscle-ups.

- **Squats**: From assisted or incline squats, you can move to free squats, then to jump squats and finally to pistol squats.

Benefits of Progressions:

1. **CONSTANT DEVELOPMENT**: Progressions ensure that the body continues to be stimulated in new and challenging ways, avoiding stalemates in training.

2. **Customized Adaptation**: Each individual can progress at his or her own pace, tailoring the progression to his or her needs and goals.

3. **Safety**: Proceeding in stages minimizes the risk of overloading muscles or joints.

In the next chapter, 4.2 "Modifying Exercises to Increase Intensity," we will explore specific techniques for intensifying exercises, allowing practitioners to constantly adapt their training regimen for continued growth. This understanding of progressions and modifications is crucial to maintaining a constant level of challenge and interest, avoiding stagnation in the fitness journey.

4.2 Modify exercises to increase intensity

Modifying exercises to increase intensity is a key strategy in calisthenics, allowing practitioners to adapt workouts to their evolving abilities and maintain a constant challenge for the body. Increasing intensity not only pushes muscles beyond their current limits, promoting growth, but also improves endurance and confidence. In this chapter, we will explore some techniques for increasing exercise intensity, setting the stage for the next section, 4.3 "Using your body weight to increase challenge."

Increasing Repetitions and Sets: One of the easiest ways to increase intensity is to increase the number of repetitions per set or add extra sets. This technique requires the muscles to work longer, improving endurance and strength over time.

However, it is essential to maintain good form even while increasing repetitions to avoid injury.

Shorten Rest Time: By shortening the rest time between sets or exercises, the body has less time to recover, testing muscular and cardiovascular endurance. This technique can be especially effective in combination with high-intensity circuits.

Taking advantage of Time Under Tension: Time under tension refers to how long the muscles are under load during an exercise. To increase intensity, deliberately slow down each repetition, keeping the muscles contracted longer. This can be done in both the concentric (push/pull) and eccentric (release) phases. For example, in push-ups, slowly descend toward the ground before quickly returning to the starting position.

Add Plyometric Movements: Plyometric exercises are explosive movements such as jumps or sprints. Incorporating plyometric movements into push-ups, squats or lunges significantly increases the intensity, requiring quick and powerful use of the muscles.

Use Variants: Many exercises have variations that can make them more challenging. For example, going from a standard plank to a plank with leg lifts increases the difficulty. Similarly, pull-ups can be made more difficult with wider holds or by adding extra weight through ballasts or special vests.

Taking advantage of Instability: Exercising on unstable surfaces such as a soft mat, fitball or suspended bar can increase intensity by forcing the body to work harder to maintain balance. This type of challenge further develops the stabilizing muscles.

Perform High Intensity Circuits: Combining several exercises in a circuit without breaks between them keeps the heart rate high and maximizes the effectiveness of the workout. This type of training improves both muscular and cardiovascular endurance.

By modifying exercises in these ways, practitioners can keep training challenging and progressive. In the next chapter, 4.3 "Using One's Body Weight to Increase the Challenge," we will explore how to make full use of body weight to take training to the next level, without resorting to expensive or sophisticated equipment.

4.3 Use your own body weight to increase the challenge

The use of body weight is a key principle of calisthenics. The versatility of this type of training allows for increased challenge without additional equipment. Using body weight intelligently allows the workout to become more and more challenging, providing continuous and safe progression. In this chapter, we will explore how to use your weight to consistently challenge your muscles, linking to Section 4.4, "Advanced Exercises and Their Benefits," which will further explore this challenge with more complex movements.

Lever Change: Lever change changes the body position to shift more weight to the target muscles. For example, during push-ups, placing the feet on an elevated surface increases intensity because the body weight is distributed closer to the shoulders. In the same way, moving the hands to the feet in planks increases the intensity on the core.

Unilateral Balancing: Working on only one limb at a time adds considerable challenge to the exercise. Single leg squats (pistol squats), one-arm push-ups and one-handed pull-ups require tremendous strength and increased body control. Forward lunges (lunges) also work the legs individually, improving balance.

Time Manipulation: Slowing down the execution of an exercise keeps muscles under tension longer, increasing exertion. Similarly, static pauses in a position of maximum effort (e.g., holding a push-up halfway down) require tremendous muscle endurance.

Integration of Dynamic Movements: Dynamic movements such as jumping jacks (jump lunges, jump squats) add a plyometric element that improves muscle power. This requires a rapid change between contraction and extension of muscles, maximizing muscle activation.

Exploiting Instability: Exercises on unstable surfaces, such as a soft mat or with limbs on fitness balls, challenge the stabilizing muscles as the main ones perform the movement. Maintaining balance during a single movement also becomes more challenging.

Isometrics: Isometric exercises, such as holding a fixed position, use body weight to strengthen muscles without dynamic movements. Plank, wall sit and L-sit are examples of effective isometrics.

Core incorporation: Many exercises require core activation to maintain balance. Movements such as pull-ups with bent knees or push-ups with leg lifts involve the core, making the exercise more challenging and complete.

With these techniques, practitioners can take full advantage of their own weight to intensify their training without the need for external equipment. This progressive approach paves the way for the next section, 4.4 "Advanced Exercises and Their Benefits," where we will explore some of the more challenging exercises in calisthenics. These exercises are a natural progression for those seeking a greater challenge and are designed to build strength, endurance, and mobility.

4.4 Advanced exercises and their benefits

Calisthenics is known for its advanced exercises, which require a high level of strength, balance, body control and flexibility. These exercises are a natural step after mastering the basics and can offer a rewarding challenge for those seeking to take their training to the next level. By exploring these exercises, practitioners will be able to understand the benefits of each and find ways to incorporate them into their routines, setting the stage for Section 4.5, "Monitoring Progress and Adapting Training."

Front Lever: The front lever involves holding the body in a horizontal position while holding onto a bar with outstretched arms. This exercise requires great strength in the back, core and arms. It strengthens the back muscles, abdominals and improves grip.

Human Flag: The human flag requires supporting the body horizontally from a vertical bar, with one hand on top and one hand underneath. Shoulder and core strength is essential for this exercise, which develops stability and power throughout the body.

Muscle-up: The muscle-up combines a pull-up and a dip, requiring the practitioner to pull himself over a bar and then push his body upward. Benefits include significant strength in the arms and back, with improved coordination in movements.

Handstand Push-up: This exercise involves doing push-ups while standing upright on the hands. It requires high strength in the shoulders, arms and core. Benefits include increased upper body strength and improved coordination.

Back Lever: Similar to the front lever but with the body facing down, the back lever primarily strengthens the shoulders and core. It is an excellent progression for developing shoulder mobility.

Incorporating these advanced exercises takes time and practice, but offers significant benefits in strength, mobility, and coordination. By incorporating appropriate progressions, practitioners can gradually approach these challenging movements, ensuring that they have a solid foundation of strength and technique.

The next chapter, 4.5 "Monitoring Progress and Adapting Training," will show how to track development in calisthenics and adjust the program based on progress. This will ensure steady improvement and motivate practitioners toward new goals, avoiding the frustrations associated with stalls and stagnation in the training path.

4.5 Monitor progress and adapt training

Monitoring progress and adapting training is a key aspect of ensuring continuous improvement in calisthenics. Without regular evaluation of progress, it is difficult to identify areas for improvement or correct imbalances in the training regimen. In this section, we will examine strategies for tracking development and adapting the program, setting the stage for the next chapter, 5.1 "Creating a Weekly Training Program."

Establish Clear Metrics: To effectively monitor progress, it is essential to establish specific metrics to measure. This may include number of repetitions, time held in a position, or number of sets completed. Other metrics may be flexibility, endurance, or body weight. Choose metrics relevant to your goals.

Keeping a Training Journal: A training journal is a simple but effective tool for tracking progress. By noting each session, you can monitor how your performance changes over time. This allows you to identify positive or negative trends and adjust your program accordingly.

Photographs of Progress: Taking periodic photographs of physical progress provides visual feedback on the transformation of the body. Because changes are gradual, they are often difficult to notice on a daily basis, but photographs can show tangible improvements.

Periodic Assessment Tests: Including regular tests to assess strength, endurance and flexibility allows you to measure progress in a structured way. For example, performing a monthly test of push-ups or pull-ups will help you see if you are making progress toward your goals.

Workout Feedback: After each session, evaluate how you feel. Are there exercises that are particularly challenging? Do you feel pain or discomfort in certain areas? This self-assessment can help identify where you might need to improve technique or intensity distribution.

Adapt Training: Based on the data you collect, you can adapt your training to make it more effective. If you notice consistent progress in certain areas, it may be time to increase the intensity or introduce more challenging variations. Conversely, if you detect persistent difficulties in certain exercises, it may be beneficial to return to easier variations or incorporate supportive exercises.

Variety in Training: Regularly incorporating new exercises and variations keeps the program challenging and prevents boredom and muscle overload. This is also a good way to test your skills in new situations and identify areas for improvement.

Consistency and Patience: Progress in calisthenics takes time and patience. Don't be discouraged by slower-than-expected progress; maintain consistency in your workouts and dedication to technique. This will bring solid and lasting results.

The next chapter, 5.1 "Creating a Weekly Training Program," will guide readers in building a structured plan that integrates all the information gathered through progress monitoring. A well-designed weekly program will ensure a steady path toward improving and optimizing personal capabilities.

Chapter 5: Workouts and Model Programs

5.1 Create a weekly training program

A well-structured weekly training program is essential for maintaining consistency, motivation, and steady progress in calisthenics. Planning workouts throughout the week ensures that all muscle groups are trained in a balanced manner and allows adequate recovery between sessions. This chapter will provide guidance for creating an effective weekly program, introducing the next chapter, 5.2 "Examples of Daily Routines," with more specific suggestions.

Determine Goals: Before planning your weekly program, identify your short- and long-term goals. Do you want to increase strength, develop new skills, or lose weight? Each goal will require a different approach in terms of intensity, repetitions, and variety of exercises.

Plan Frequency of Workouts: For beginners, two or three sessions per week may be sufficient to build a solid foundation. As you gain strength and endurance, the frequency can be increased to four or five days a week. It is essential to plan rest days to allow the body to recover, avoiding the risk of overtraining.

Distribute Muscle Groups: Dividing muscle groups between sessions ensures a balanced workout. A common example is the upper-lower system, where one day is devoted to the upper body (push-ups, pull-ups) and the next to the lower body (squats, lunges). Another option is to devote each day to a specific region, such as shoulders, back, core, or legs.

Incorporate Progressions: To achieve your goals, include progressions in your weekly routines. This may mean increasing the number of repetitions, adding more complex variations or reducing the rest time between sets. Progressions should be gradual, allowing the body to adapt to a higher level of intensity.

Integrate Cardio: Cardio is an important component of cardiovascular health and weight management. Examples include running, jumping rope, or high-intensity circuits. Devote at least one or two days to these activities, or full on days when you work the lower body.

Stretching and Mobility: Be sure to include stretching and mobility sessions at the end of each workout or as a separate session. This helps keep muscles supple and reduces the risk of injury.

Evaluation and Adaptation: Record performance and evaluate progress each week to identify what works and what needs improvement. If an exercise is too easy, increase the intensity. If a muscle group fatigues quickly, it may need more rest.

Example Schedule: An example of a weekly program might be:

- **Monday**: upper body - pull-ups, dips, push-ups
- **Tuesday**: lower body - squats, lunges, calf raises
- **Wednesday**: Cardio - running or HIIT circuit
- **Thursday**: Core - planks, crunches, leg raises

- **Friday**: Whole body - combination of upper, lower and core
- **Saturday**: Active rest - stretching, yoga, walking
- **Sunday**: full rest

In the next chapter, 5.2 "Examples of Daily Routines," we will provide details on individual training sessions to show how a typical day can be structured, ensuring that each session is balanced, effective and engaging.

5.2 Examples of daily routines

A well-designed daily routine is the key to making each training session productive, balanced and engaging. In calisthenics, daily routines should be tailored to each individual's goals and skill level. In this chapter, we will look at some examples of daily routines to train different parts of the body, connecting this with the next section, 5.3 "Variations to Prevent Monotony," which will explore how to keep training interesting at all times.

Upper Body Routine: This routine focuses on strengthening upper body muscles such as pecs, shoulders and back, including triceps and biceps.

1. Warm-up: About 10 minutes warm-up with dynamic movements such as shoulder rotations, torso rotations, and light jumps to prepare muscles and joints.
2. **Main Exercises**:
    - Pull-ups: 3 sets of 8-10 repetitions

- Dips: 3 sets of 10-12 repetitions

- Diamond Push-ups: 3 sets of 12-15 repetitions

- Plank: 3 sets of 30-45 seconds

3. **Cooling and Stretching**: Stretching the muscles involved for 5-10 minutes to promote recovery.

Lower Body Routine: This routine is designed to strengthen the legs, focusing on the quadriceps, glutes, and hamstrings.

1. **Warm-up**: 10 minutes of dynamic exercises such as jumping jacks, hip rotations, and jumping in place.

2. **Main Exercises**:
    - Squat: 4 sets of 10-15 repetitions

- Forward Lunges: 3 sets of 12-15 repetitions per leg

- Pistol Squat (assisted): 3 sets of 6-8 repetitions per leg

- Calf Raises: 3 sets of 15-20 repetitions

   3. **Cooling and Stretching**: Stretching leg muscles for 5-10 minutes.

Core Routine: This routine focuses on strengthening the core, which is essential for balance, stability and support of the body during other exercises.

   1. **Warm-up**: 10 minutes of dynamic movements such as torso twists and light jumps.
   2. **Main Exercises**:
      - Side Plank: 3 sets of 20-30 seconds per side

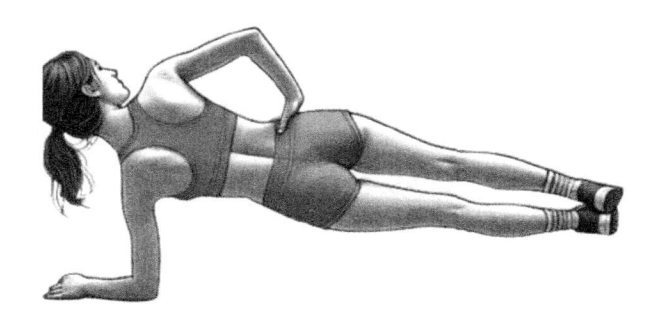

- Leg Raises: 3 sets of 10-12 repetitions

- Bicycle Crunch: 3 sets of 12-15 repetitions

- Mountain Climbers: 3 sets of 15-20 repetitions per leg

3. **Cooling and Stretching**: 5-10 minutes of core stretching.

Complete Routine: A complete routine involves all parts of the body for a balanced workout.

1. **Warm-up**: 10 minutes of dynamic exercises such as jumping jacks, arm spins, and running in place.

2. **Main Exercises**:
   - Push-ups: 3 sets of 12-15 repetitions
   - Pull-ups: 3 sets of 8-10 repetitions
   - Squat: 3 sets of 12-15 repetitions
   - Plank: 3 sets of 30-45 seconds

3. **Cooling and Stretching**: 5-10 minutes of stretching for all parts of the body.

In the next chapter, 5.3 "Variations to Prevent Monotony," we will discuss how to vary daily routines to keep training interesting and engaging at all times, ensuring continuous progress without falling into boredom or repetitiveness.

5.3 Variations to prevent monotony

In calisthenics, monotony can easily infiltrate when the same exercises and routines are repeated every day. This repetitiveness can lead to boredom, loss of motivation and even stalled progress. To keep training fresh and engaging, it is essential to introduce variation. In this chapter, we will explore effective strategies to avoid monotony, preparing us for the next section, 5.4 "Adapting Training to Your Needs," in which we will delve into how to make training personalized and satisfying.

Vary the Type of Exercise: Including different variations of each exercise is one of the most effective strategies for keeping the workout interesting. For example, instead of always performing standard push-ups, alternate variations such as diamond push-ups, plyometric push-ups or incline push-ups. The same principle applies to pull-ups, squats and planks, where each exercise offers many challenging variations.

Circuit Workouts: A circuit involves a series of different exercises performed consecutively with little or no rest. This form of training keeps the heart rate up and challenges the muscles in different ways. Alternating upper-body, lower-body and core exercises during a circuit provides a complete and engaging workout.

Tabata and **HIIT**: Tabata and HIIT (High-Intensity Interval Training) are training protocols that alternate short periods of high-intensity work with shorter periods of rest. They are ideal for keeping training dynamic and making the most of available time.

Advanced Exercises as a Goal: Including an advanced exercise in your weekly routine as a goal can add a new challenge. Movements such as planche, muscle-ups or pistol squats offer a new level of difficulty and can provide motivation as you work toward achieving them.

Unilateral Exercises: Unilateral exercises, which focus on one side of the body at a time, add an element of challenge and help correct muscle imbalances. Lunges, step-ups and one-arm push-ups are examples of unilateral exercises that add variety.

Targeted Progressions: Following targeted progressions for each exercise is a great way to ensure continued growth and variation. For example, work on easier variations of an advanced exercise until you master the ultimate one, such as practicing dips with assistance until you reach muscle-up.

Add Cardio Elements: Integrating cardio elements, such as running, jumping rope or burpees, helps keep the intensity of the workout high and the stimulus varied.

Active Recovery Days: Including active recovery days with activities as diverse as yoga, Pilates or simple walking can help relax tired muscles and offer a break from more intense strength routines.

Using these strategies, you can avoid monotony and maintain enthusiasm during your calisthenics sessions. In the next chapter, 5.4 "Tailoring Your Workout to Your Needs," we will discuss how to customize your workout program according to your goals, fitness level, and personal preferences, ensuring that each individual can maximize results and enjoy their fitness journey.

5.4 Adapt training to your needs

Calisthenics is extremely versatile, making it easy to adapt workouts to meet personal needs. Each individual has different goals, physical conditions and preferences, and finding the right balance between these variables is critical to developing an effective and sustainable training program. In this section, we will examine how to customize training, setting the stage for the next chapter, 5.5 "Tips for Staying Consistent."

Define Personal Goals: The first step in tailoring your training program is to clearly establish your personal goals. Do you want to build muscle mass, improve endurance, lose weight, or develop new skills? Each goal requires a different approach in terms of exercise, intensity, and frequency.

- **Muscle mass**: Focus on compound exercises, such as push-ups, pull-ups, and squats, that involve different muscle groups, with progressions that add intensity and more challenging variations.
- **Endurance**: Circuit training and high-intensity routines are ideal for improving muscular and cardiovascular endurance.
- **Weight loss**: A mix of strength and cardio exercises, combined with a balanced eating plan, can help burn fat while maintaining muscle mass.

- **New skills**: Identify specific exercises such as planche or muscle-up and work on progressions to reach the desired level.

Assess Skill Level: Know your skill level and work on appropriate progressions. If you are a beginner, start with simpler exercises and gradually increase the difficulty. The advanced can instead focus on more complex variations or add weight.

Consider Physical Limitations: If you have injuries or medical conditions, adapt your training to avoid overloading. Reduce the intensity or opt for exercises with less impact on joints, such as planks on elbows instead of hands, or assisted lunges.

Customizing Frequency: Available time is a determining factor for many. If you are short on time, focus on shorter but intense workouts. If you have more time, spread out your sessions to include specific days for stretching and recovery.

Add Variety: Integrate exercises that involve different parts of the body to avoid overloading a single region. Variations of push-ups, pull-ups and squats provide opportunities to diversify workouts.

Manage Recovery: Allocate rest days between sessions to give muscles time to repair and grow. If fatigue occurs, replace strength sessions with low-impact exercises such as stretching or yoga.

Monitor and Adapt: Keep track of progress and regularly evaluate the effectiveness of the program. If an exercise becomes too easy, switch to a more challenging variation. If motivation wanes, try new activities or exercises to rekindle interest.

The next chapter, 5.5 "Tips for Staying Consistent," will provide practical suggestions for maintaining motivation and building a sustainable routine, ensuring that your journey in calisthenics continues to be challenging and satisfying.

5.5 Tips for staying consistent

Maintaining a consistent routine is one of the biggest challenges for those embarking on a fitness journey. Even with the clearest goals and careful planning, motivation can fluctuate, leading to loss of momentum. This section will explore some strategies for staying consistent and committed over time, paving the way for the next chapter, 6.1 "Fundamentals of Fitness Nutrition," where the dietary principles that support training will be discussed.

Establish a Fixed Routine: Creating a regular, predictable routine is essential to maintaining commitment. Assign specific days and times for each workout, as if it were a fixed appointment. Consistency over time will reinforce the habit, making it less likely to skip a session.

Keeping a Training Journal: Documenting each session helps monitor progress and maintain a sense of accountability. Noting sets, repetitions and variations of exercises provides a clear view of improvements and can reveal which areas need more attention.

Celebrating Victories: Recognizing accomplishments, even small ones, is critical to staying motivated. Celebrate when you can do an extra push-up, complete a new variation, or improve your time in planks. Every progress is a step toward your goals.

Finding a Training Partner: Training with a friend or group can provide support and encourage mutual accountability. A workout partner can make sessions more fun and help you stay motivated even on less energetic days.

Vary the Routine: Periodically changing exercises and trying new challenges prevents boredom and keeps interest alive. Introduce new exercises, variations or programs to energize your routine.

Flexibility in Planning: Don't feel guilty if you miss a day. Life can be unpredictable, but be sure to get right back on track. If you can't train one day, opt for a shorter session or rearrange your schedule.

Visualizing Goals: Visualizing your goals and envisioning desired outcomes helps keep you motivated. Create a list of goals achieved and future goals, reviewing them periodically to remind yourself why you started this journey.

Avoid Overload: Listen to your body and don't overtrain. Overloading can lead to injuries and injuries. Be sure to incorporate rest days and active recovery into your routine to give your muscles time to regenerate.

Adequate Nutrition: Proper nutrition is crucial to sustaining your efforts. Without the necessary energy, it becomes more difficult to train consistently. In the next chapter, 6.1 "Fundamentals of Fitness Nutrition," we will examine how a balanced diet can optimize your workout results and keep you fit.

Staying consistent in calisthenics is a personal journey that requires patience, dedication and strategy. By following these tips, you will be able to maintain a steady path toward your fitness goals, meeting challenges with resilience and adaptability.

Chapter 6: Nutrition for Calisthenics.

6.1 Fundamentals of nutrition for fitness

Nutrition plays a crucial role in sustaining and maximizing training results. Without a proper nutrition plan, even the most intense fitness regimen can lead to limited results. The principles of proper fitness nutrition are essential for sustaining energy levels, promoting muscle recovery, and promoting growth. In this section, we will explore the fundamentals of fitness nutrition, linking to Chapter 6.2 "Foods to Prefer and Avoid" below.

Importance of Protein: Protein is essential for building and repairing muscle tissue. Protein sources can be both animal and plant-based and include lean meat, fish, eggs, dairy products, legumes, and nuts. Consuming an adequate amount of protein, generally between 1.2 and 2 grams per kilogram of body weight, helps support muscle growth and prevent loss of lean mass during weight loss.

Carbohydrates for Energy: Carbohydrates are the main source of energy for the body during exercise. Complex carbohydrates such as whole grains, rice, potatoes, and starchy vegetables provide a steady release of energy. Before a workout, it is helpful to take a serving of carbohydrates to ensure that you have sufficient energy reserves.

Healthy Fats: Fats are often misunderstood, but they are important for proper hormone function and overall health. Sources of healthy fats include avocados, nuts, seeds, fatty fish, and olive oil. These foods can help reduce inflammation and provide energy during low-impact workouts.

Hydration: Staying hydrated is critical to sustaining physical performance and concentration. Drinking water before, during and after training keeps the body well lubricated and helps prevent muscle cramps and fatigue. In more intense or longer workouts, you may consider taking electrolytes to replace those lost through sweating.

Meal Timing: Meal timing can affect training effectiveness and recovery. Consuming a meal with carbohydrates and protein about 2-3 hours before training provides energy, while a small snack 30 minutes before can help sustain performance. After training, a meal rich in protein and carbohydrates is essential to promote protein synthesis and replenish glycogen stores.

Micronutrients: Vitamins and minerals are essential for general well-being and muscle function. Fruits, vegetables, nuts, and seeds provide essential vitamins and minerals such as vitamin C, magnesium, potassium, and calcium. Incorporating a variety of fresh foods into the diet can help prevent deficiencies.

Avoiding Excesses: It is important to avoid overindulging in refined sugars, processed foods, and alcohol, which can negatively affect energy, recovery, and overall health.

In the next chapter, 6.2 "Foods to Prefer and Avoid," we will delve into which foods to incorporate into the diet and which to limit, providing a practical guide to optimizing the food plan for training.

6.2 Foods to prefer and avoid

A balanced diet consisting of high-quality foods is essential to optimize health and support training in calisthenics. Some foods provide valuable nutrients that enhance performance, while others can be harmful if consumed in excess. In this chapter, we will discuss which foods to prefer for effective training and which to avoid, introducing the next chapter 6.3, "Meal Planning to Optimize Performance."

Foods to Prefer:

1. **Lean Protein:**

    - **Lean meats** such as chicken, turkey, and lean red meat are excellent sources of protein for muscle growth.

    - **Fish** such as salmon, tuna, and mackerel provide not only protein but also beneficial omega-3 fatty acids.

    - **Legumes** such as lentils, beans and chickpeas are rich in protein and fiber.

2. **Complex Carbohydrates:**

    - **Whole grains** such as oats, quinoa, brown rice, and spelt offer a slow and steady release of energy.

    - **Sweet potatoes** and **pumpkin** provide carbohydrates with high vitamin and mineral content.

- **Fruits** such as bananas and berries contain natural sugars and electrolytes, which are ideal for recovery.

3. **Healthy Fats**:
   - **Olive oil** and **avocados** are rich in monounsaturated fats that support cardiovascular health.
   - **Seeds and nuts** such as almonds, chia seeds, and flax seeds are excellent sources of fat, fiber, and protein.

4. **Green Leafy Vegetables**:
   - Spinach, kale, chard, and other leafy green vegetables contain essential vitamins and minerals such as iron, calcium, and magnesium.

5. **Water and Natural Electrolyte Beverages**:
   - Water is the primary beverage for maintaining hydration.
   - Coconut water and herbal teas are good alternatives for adding electrolytes without added sugar.

Foods to Avoid:

1. **Refined Sugars**:
   - Sugary drinks, sweets and baked goods can cause blood sugar spikes, leading to a rapid drop in energy.

2. **Processed Foods**:

- Packaged snacks, fast foods and processed meats often contain high amounts of saturated fats, sugars and additives.

3. **Fat Trans**:
    - Hydrogenated oils used in many baked goods and fried foods are harmful to cardiovascular health.

4. **Alcohol**:
    - Alcohol can interfere with muscle recovery and sleep quality, negatively affecting performance.

5. **Excess Salt**:
    - Foods high in sodium, such as chips and cold cuts, can cause water retention and affect blood pressure.

Choosing the right foods can make a significant difference in training quality and recovery. In the next chapter, 6.3 "Meal Planning to Optimize Performance," we will explore how to organize your meals and snacks to better support your journey in calisthenics, ensuring that your body consistently gets the nutrients it needs.

6.3 Meal planning to optimize performance

Meal planning is critical to provide the body with the energy and nutrients it needs for effective training and optimal recovery. A well-structured meal plan allows you to avoid energy surges, maintain an active metabolism, and support muscle growth. In this section, we will look at how to organize meals to meet training needs, introducing the next section 6.4, "Supplements: use and advice," which focuses on supplements to fill nutritional gaps.

Macronutrient Distribution: The proper proportion of protein, carbohydrates, and fat varies according to individual goals and type of training. In general:

- **Protein**: It should account for 20-30% of daily caloric intake, as it is essential for muscle growth and recovery.
- **Carbohydrates**: They provide the primary energy for exercise and should account for 40-60% of daily calories.
- **Fats**: About 20-30% of calories should come from healthy fats, which are crucial for metabolism and hormone function.

Pre-Workout Meals: Consuming a pre-workout meal provides the energy needed to sustain the most demanding sessions.

- **Timing**: A main meal 2-3 hours before training allows the body to absorb nutrients, while a light snack 30-60 minutes before provides immediate energy.
- **Composition**: A combination of complex carbohydrates and protein is ideal. For example, a meal might include brown rice with chicken and vegetables, while a snack might consist of a fruit with yogurt.

Post-Workout Meals: A post-workout meal helps restore energy reserves and promote protein synthesis.

- **Timing**: Eating within 30 to 60 minutes after training is essential to maximize recovery.

- **Composition**: A combination of carbohydrates and protein accelerates muscle repair. An example would be a protein shake with fruit and oats or an omelet with whole wheat bread and vegetables.

Planning Main Meals: Make sure each main meal contains a source of protein, complex carbohydrates and healthy fats.

- **Breakfast**: Oats with nuts and fruit or eggs with whole wheat bread and avocado.
- **Lunch**: Salad with grilled chicken, quinoa and seeds.
- **Dinner**: Fish with brown rice, steamed vegetables and olive oil.

Snacks between Meals: Snacks can keep energy levels steady and prevent hunger.

- **Dried Fruits and Seeds**: Rich in healthy fats, protein and minerals.
- **Fresh Fruit**: Provides natural sugars and electrolytes.
- **Protein Bars or Shakes**: Convenient and nutritious to support protein levels.

Hydration: Drinking water throughout the day is essential to maintain physical performance. A minimum of 2 liters per day is recommended, increasing during intense workouts.

Effective meal planning can support training in calisthenics by optimizing energy and recovery. In the next chapter, 6.4 "Supplements: use and advice," we will explore the role of supplements in the diet, when they can be useful, and how to select them based on specific goals.

6.4 Supplements: use and advice

Dietary supplements can be useful for filling nutritional gaps or improving performance and recovery. However, they should be used strategically, as a complement to a balanced diet and not as substitutes for natural foods. This section will explore how to use supplements safely and effectively, linking to the next section 6.5, "Keeping a Food Diary."

Protein Powder: Protein is critical for muscle growth and tissue repair.

- **Usage**: They can be used to achieve daily protein intake when it is not possible to do so by diet alone.
- **Types**: Whey protein (whey) is easily digested and ideal post-workout. Plant proteins, such as soy or pea proteins, are good alternatives for those on a vegan diet or with lactose intolerances.
- **Dosage**: Generally, one serving of 20-30 grams is sufficient.

Creatine: Creatine is a popular supplement for increasing strength and power.

- **Benefits**: Increases phosphocreatine reserves in muscles, improving the ability to perform high-intensity exercise.
- **Usage**: Take 3-5 grams daily, ideally after training, in combination with simple carbohydrates to maximize absorption.

Ramified Amino Acids (BCAAs): BCAAs are composed of leucine, isoleucine and valine, three essential amino acids.

- **Benefits**: Can reduce muscle fatigue and improve recovery.
- **Usage**: About 5 to 10 grams during or after training, especially for those on a low-calorie diet. They can be contained in rusks, bresaola or fresh peas, for example.

Multivitamins: Multivitamins help prevent deficiencies of essential vitamins and minerals.

- **Benefits**: Supports immune function, metabolism, and overall health.
- **Usage**: Take a daily multivitamin supplement, preferably with a meal to improve absorption.

Omega-3: Omega-3 fatty acids are essential for cardiovascular and cognitive health.

- **Benefits**: Reduces inflammation, improves joint health and promotes brain function.
- **Usage**: 1-2 grams daily, preferably in the form of fish oil or algae.

Beta-Alanine: Beta-alanine is an amino acid that can increase muscle endurance.

- **Benefits**: Reduces lactic acid buildup in muscles during intense exercises.
- **Usage**: Take 2-5 grams daily, divided into smaller doses to minimize tingling sensation.

General Considerations:

- **Consult a Professional**: Before starting any supplement, consult a dietitian or physician to make sure it is right for you.

- **Quality**: Choose products from reputable brands and tested by third parties to ensure purity.

- **Moderation**: Supplements should be used as an addition to the diet, not as meal replacements.

In the next chapter, 6.5 "Keeping a Food Diary," we will discuss how to track eating habits to ensure consistent and adequate nutrient intake, monitoring the impact of supplements on progress and making adjustments as needed.

6.5 Maintaining a food diary

Keeping a food diary is an effective way to keep track of nutritional habits, helping to understand the link between diet and physical performance. By documenting daily meals and feelings, it is possible to gain a clear view of eating behaviors, identifying areas for improvement. In this chapter, we will discuss the importance of the food diary and how to use it, introducing the next section 7.1, "Relationship between Calisthenics and Weight Loss," to understand how nutrition can support weight loss.

Benefits of the Food Diary:

1. **Food Awareness:**
   - Recording what you eat helps you develop a greater awareness of portion sizes, eating habits and daily choices, promoting healthier behaviors.

2. **Identification of Patterns:**
   - Documenting meals over weeks can reveal eating patterns that lead to specific outcomes, such as improved energy or fatigue.

3. **Monitoring Nutrient Intake:**
   - Keeping track of protein, carbohydrate, fat, and micronutrient intake helps to ensure that the diet is balanced and suitable for the goals.

4. **Weight Management:**
   - A food diary makes it easier to monitor total calorie intake and unnecessary snacks, helping to manage weight.

How to Start a Food Diary:

1. **Format:**
   - A journal can be kept on paper or through dedicated apps. The important thing is to find a format that is convenient and practical for daily use.

2. **Details to Include:**
   - Date and time of each meal or snack
   - Foods consumed and quantity

- Method of cooking (boiled, grilled, fried, etc.).
- Sensations before and after the meal (hunger, satiety, energy)
- Notes on particular habits, such as emotional hunger or the need for dessert

3. **Specific Goals**:
   - Set clear goals about what you want to achieve by monitoring your diet. For example, improve protein intake, limit added sugars, or increase vegetable consumption.

Data Analysis:

1. **Assessing Progress**:
   - Compare weekly data to assess whether you are achieving the goals you set. This helps you stay accountable and identify areas for improvement.

2. **Adjusting the Diet**:
   - If you notice negative patterns, such as low protein intake or excessive snack consumption, adjust the food plan to correct them.

3. **Monitoring Physical Performance**:
   - Note how changes in diet affect energy, mood, and performance in workouts. These data are valuable for optimizing nutrition.

Engaging a Professional:

- If necessary, work with a nutritionist to analyze the data and develop a customized diet plan that meets your specific needs.

The food diary provides a clear overview of nutritional behaviors and their consequences, helping to make more informed and targeted choices. In the next chapter, 7.1 "Relationship between Calisthenics and Weight Loss," we will examine how calisthenics and nutrition can work together to facilitate healthy and sustainable weight loss.

Chapter 7: Weight Management and Body Composition

7.1 Relationship between Calisthenics and weight loss

Calisthenics is a form of exercise that uses body weight to build strength, endurance and flexibility. In addition to its functional benefits, it is an effective method for weight loss because it engages the entire body in exercises that increase metabolism and help burn calories. In this chapter, we will discuss how calisthenics is closely related to weight loss and why it is an excellent choice for those who want to improve body composition, introducing the next section 7.2, "Methods for Measuring Body Composition."

High Intensity Workouts: Many calisthenics routines are structured as circuit or high-intensity interval training (HIIT) workouts, which increase heart rate and maintain high caloric expenditure.

- **Circuits**: Circuit workouts alternate exercises for different muscle groups with short breaks. This alternation keeps metabolism elevated, leading to higher calorie consumption.
- **HIIT**: Calisthenics lends itself well to exercises such as burpees, push-ups and squats that can be performed in quick succession, alternating short periods of intense work with breaks.

Here is a detailed HIIT routine you can try:

Heating:

- 3 minutes of jogging in place to increase heart rate and prepare muscles for activity.

HIIT circuit:

- **Sprint:** 30 seconds of running at maximum speed.
- **Recovery:** 90 seconds of brisk walking or light jogging.
- **Jump Squats:** 30 seconds to stimulate leg muscles.
- **Recovery:** 90 seconds of brisk walking or light jogging.
- **Burpees:** 30 seconds to engage the whole body.
- **Recovery:** 90 seconds of brisk walking or light jogging.
- **Mountain Climbers:** 30 seconds to strengthen core and shoulders.
- **Recovery:** 90 seconds of brisk walking or light jogging.

Repetition:

- Repeat the entire cycle 3-5 times depending on your fitness level.

Defatigue:

- Conclude with 3 minutes of dynamic stretching for major muscle groups, including quadriceps, ischiocrucials, shoulders and back, to prevent soreness and improve flexibility.

This type of workout is intense and helps burn many calories in a short time, improving both cardiovascular endurance and muscular strength. Be sure to hydrate well and stretch properly to avoid injury.

Increase in Muscle Mass: Increasing muscle mass is closely related to weight loss.

- **Basal Metabolism**: By increasing muscle mass, basal metabolism (resting energy expenditure) increases, helping you burn more calories even when you are not working out.
- **Compound Exercises**: Compound exercises, such as pull-ups and squats, involve large muscle groups, stimulating greater muscle growth than isolated exercises.

Core Involvement: Calisthenics emphasizes core involvement in almost all exercises.

- **Stability**: A strong core improves stability, allowing more complex exercises involving greater caloric expenditure to be performed.
- **Planks and Variants**: Exercises such as planks, leg raises and L-sits strengthen the core, reducing abdominal fat accumulation.

Free Body Exercises: Free body exercises offer some key benefits for weight loss.

- **Accessibility**: They can be performed almost anywhere, eliminating excuses related to equipment or access to gyms.
- **Progression**: Easier variations allow you to develop strength gradually, while more difficult variations keep the challenge and intensity constant.

Holistic Approach: Calisthenics promotes a holistic approach to weight loss, working on the whole body.

- **Combine Strength and Cardio**: Strength exercises can be combined with cardiovascular exercises in a complete routine that burns calories and builds muscle mass.

- **Sustainability**: The emphasis on using body weight makes calisthenics sustainable for most people by encouraging regular and consistent physical activity.

Combination with Nutrition: Calisthenics, along with a balanced diet, can be a powerful tool for weight loss.

- **Protein Intake**: Protein is critical to support muscle growth and fat loss.

- **Calorie Balance**: Maintaining a negative calorie balance, where calories burned exceed calories consumed, is essential for weight loss.

In the next chapter, 7.2 "Methods to Measure Body Composition," we will look at how to monitor physical changes to assess progress in weight loss and muscle mass gain, using more accurate metrics than simply measuring weight.

7.2 Methods for measuring body composition

Understanding and monitoring body composition is critical to assessing progress in weight loss and muscle mass gain. Body composition refers to the proportions of fat and lean mass in the body, and its measurement provides a more detailed picture of health than simply weight on the scale. This section will explore common methods for measuring body composition, linking to the next section 7.3, "Strategies for losing weight and gaining muscle."

Body Mass Index (BMI): Body Mass Index is a calculation that relates weight to height. Although it is a quick and widely used measure, BMI does not account for the difference between muscle mass and body fat.

- **Calculation**: BMI = Weight (kg) / Height² (m)
- **Limitations**: Does not distinguish between fat and muscle mass, being less accurate for athletes or individuals with significant muscle mass.

Plicometry: Plicometry is a method that measures the thickness of subcutaneous fat in different parts of the body using a caliper called a plicometer.

- **Procedures**: Specific points such as abdomen, thigh, biceps, and triceps are measured and then formulas are used to estimate body fat percentage.
- **Accuracy**: Requires practice and experience, but offers fairly accurate results if done correctly.

Impedance testing: Bioimpedance analyzes body composition by sending a low-intensity electric current through the body.

- **Procedures**: The subject stands on a special scale or holds sensors, which measure electrical resistance as the current passes through.
- **Accuracy**: Can be affected by hydration level and other factors, but provides quick estimates of fat mass, muscle mass, and body water.

DEXA Scan: Dual-Energy X-ray Absorptiometry (DEXA) is a method that uses X-rays to measure bone density and body composition.

- **Procedures**: The subject lies on a crib while the scanner passes over the body, generating a detailed image.
- **Accuracy**: Considered one of the most precise techniques, it clearly separates fat, muscle and bone mass.

Circumferences: Measuring the circumferences of different areas of the body provides a rough indication of changes in body composition.

- **Procedures**: Waist, hip, thigh, and arm circumferences are measured with a dressmaker's tape measure.
- **Accuracy**: Although less precise than other methods, it can help track progress over time.

Specific Weight: Hydrostatic weighing measures the weight of the body underwater, comparing it to the dry weight.

- **Procedures**: The subject is weighed while fully submerged in water, calculating body density.
- **Accuracy**: Very precise, but requires specialized equipment.

Each method has its advantages and limitations, so the choice depends on available resources and specific goals. In the next chapter, 7.3 "Strategies to Lose Weight and Gain Muscle," we will discuss practical tactics that combine training and nutrition to improve body composition, ensuring a balanced and sustainable path to physical transformation.

7.3 Strategies for losing weight and gaining muscle

Losing weight and gaining muscle are two closely related goals, but they are often addressed separately. An effective strategy can combine targeted training with a balanced diet to achieve both results in a sustainable way. In this chapter, we will discuss some key strategies for losing weight and gaining muscle simultaneously, linking it to the next point, 7.4 "Case Study Analysis."

Caloric Balance: Caloric balance is the starting point for losing weight and gaining muscle.

- **Caloric Deficit**: Creating a caloric deficit is essential for weight loss. This means burning more calories than you consume.
- **Protein** intake: Maintaining a high protein intake (about 1.6-2.2 g per kg of body weight) helps prevent muscle loss during caloric deficit.
- **Fats and Carbohydrates**: Reduce fats and carbohydrates slightly, but do not eliminate them completely. Fats are important for hormone function, while carbohydrates provide energy for training.

Strength Training: Strength training is crucial for stimulating muscle growth and burning calories.

- **Compound Exercises**: Focus on compound exercises such as squats, deadlifts, push-ups and pull-ups. By involving multiple muscle groups, these exercises allow you to burn more calories and develop strength.

- **Progressions**: Introduce gradual progressions by increasing the load, repetitions, or difficulty of exercises to maintain muscle growth.

- **Frequency**: Weight training 3-5 times a week provides the right stimulus for muscle growth without overdoing it.

Cardio workout: Cardio can support weight loss while maintaining high caloric expenditure.

- **HIIT (High-Intensity Interval Training)**: High-intensity sessions increase metabolism and are effective for burning fat without compromising muscle mass.

- **LISS (Low-Intensity Steady State)**: Low-intensity exercise, such as walking or biking, can be a useful addition to increase caloric expenditure without overstressing the body.

Recovery and Sleep: Recovery is essential to allow the body to regenerate.

- **Sleep**: Sleeping at least 7-8 hours a night supports protein synthesis and hormone regulation.

- **Active Rest**: Including active rest days with light activities, such as stretching or yoga, can help reduce stress and promote flexibility.

Stress Management: Stress can interfere with fitness goals.

- **Stress Hormones**: Cortisol and other stress hormones can negatively affect muscle growth and promote the accumulation of abdominal fat.

- **Relaxation Techniques**: Meditation, deep breathing and relaxing hobbies can reduce the impact of stress.

Progress Monitoring: Keeping track of progress helps maintain motivation.

- **Training Diary**: Document training sessions and food intake to identify improvements and adapt strategies.
- **Photographs and Measurements**: Taking periodic photos and measurements can highlight physical changes that the scale often fails to detect.

In the next chapter, 7.4 "Analysis and Some Case Studies," we will examine how these strategies have been successfully applied through real stories, showing the progress and challenges faced during the fitness journey.

7.4 Analysis and studies of some cases

The case studies provide concrete examples of how people have applied specific strategies to lose weight and gain muscle. These stories illustrate the different challenges and solutions adopted to achieve remarkable results. In this chapter, we will look at some real cases, linking it to the next section, 7.5 "Achieving and Maintaining Ideal Weight," which will explore how to stabilize the results achieved.

Case 1: Laura - Transformation through Calisthenics and Nutrition:

Profile:

- Age: 34 years old

- **Goal**: Lose 10 kg and tone the body after pregnancy.

Approach:

- **Training**:
    - **Routine**: Focused on a calisthenics routine 3 times a week, doing circuits of compound exercises (push-ups, pull-ups, squats, planks).
    - **Progression**: Started with simplified variations of exercises to develop strength, gradually moving to more challenging variations.
- **Nutrition**:
    - **Calorie intake**: Maintained a moderate calorie deficit of about 500 kcal per day.
    - **Macronutrients**: Increased protein intake through lean sources such as chicken, fish and legumes, while reducing refined sugar intake.

Results:

- He lost 8 kg in 4 months, gaining muscle mass and improving physical endurance.
- He reported increased energy during the day and improved sleep quality.

Case 2: Mark-Strength and Fat Loss with Targeted Training:

Profile:

- Age: 45 years old
- **Goal**: Lose 50 pounds of fat while maintaining muscle mass.

Approach:

- **Training**:
  - **Routine**: Alternated strength exercises (deadlifts, pull-ups, dips) with HIIT circuits to maximize caloric expenditure.
  - **Cardio**: Added light running and brisk walking sessions 3 times a week.
- **Nutrition**:
  - **Macronutrients**: Reduced intake of refined carbohydrates, focusing on complex carbohydrates such as quinoa and oats.
  - **Protein**: Maintained a high protein intake with lean protein and shakes.

Results:

- He lost 12 kg in 5 months, with a significant reduction in abdominal fat.
- He reported having more energy and increased strength.

Case 3: Julia - Improving Body Composition:

Profile:

- Age: 29 years old
- **Goal**: To improve body composition without losing weight.

Approach:

- **Training**:

- **Routine**: He followed a strength training and calisthenics routine 4 times a week, focusing on lower body exercises (squats, lunges, step-ups).
- **Nutrition**:
  - **Calorie balance**: He maintained a caloric intake equal to his energy requirements.
  - **Macronutrients**: Increased protein and healthy fat intake.

Results:

- It increased visible muscle mass, improving strength without significant changes in weight.

These cases demonstrate that the personalized approach in training and nutrition can produce significant results. In the next chapter, 7.5 "Achieving and Maintaining Ideal Weight," we will discuss strategies to stabilize and maintain the desired weight over the long term, avoiding weight fluctuations and regain.

7.5 Achieving and maintaining ideal weight

Achieving an ideal weight is a key goal for many people embarking on a fitness journey, but maintaining it can be equally challenging. After making significant progress through training and nutrition, it is important to develop strategies to consolidate results and stabilize weight over the long term. In this chapter, we will discuss how to achieve and maintain ideal weight sustainably, linking to the next section, 8.1 "Progress Tracking Techniques."

Create a Sustainable Plan: The maintenance plan should be achievable and adaptable to lifestyle.

- **Workout Routine**: Maintain a regular routine that includes both strength exercises and cardio activities. A combination of these keeps your metabolism active and reduces your risk of regaining weight.
- **Food Flexibility**: Be realistic about diet. A plan that provides flexibility in occasional foods, but relies primarily on nutritious foods, will be more sustainable.

Setting New Goals: After reaching your desired weight, setting new goals can keep you motivated.

- **Strength or Performance Goals**: Develop new fitness goals, such as increasing the number of repetitions or learning new skills.
- **General Wellness**: Focus on aspects of wellness such as sleep quality, stress management, and mental health.

Constant Monitoring: Keeping track of progress and habits helps to quickly detect signs of possible weight regain.

- **Food Diary**: Continuing to document nutrition helps maintain awareness of eating habits.
- **Photographs and Measurements**: Taking periodic photos and measuring body circumferences can highlight changes that the scale may not show.

Prevent Fluctuations: Avoid weight fluctuations by implementing preventive strategies.

- **Portion Control**: Eating balanced portions helps avoid excess.

- **Emotional Awareness**: Identify situations that may lead to impulsive or excessive eating and find healthy alternatives to handle them.

Staying Active: Regular physical activity is essential for maintaining weight.

- **Weekly Routine**: Plan at least 150 minutes of moderate physical activity or 75 minutes of vigorous activity each week, distributing them evenly.
- **Daily Activities**: Include more movement in daily activities, such as walking more, taking the stairs and limiting time sitting.

Social Support: Having social support can be instrumental in maintaining a healthy weight.

- **Workout Partners**: Working out with a friend or group can make physical activity more fun and motivating.
- **Family and Friends**: Involve family and friends in your goals, seeking their support to maintain a healthy lifestyle.

Stress and Sleep Management: Stress and lack of sleep can interfere with weight maintenance.

- **Relaxation Techniques**: Practice meditation, progressive relaxation or other techniques to reduce stress.
- **Quality of Sleep**: Sleeping at least 7-8 hours a night improves mood and reduces hunger.

In the next chapter, 8.1 "Breathing Techniques to Improve Performance," we will discuss tools and methods for exploring different breathing techniques that are essential for optimizing oxygenation and muscle performance.

Chapter 8: Advanced Breathing and Concentration Techniques in Calisthenics.

8.1 Breathing Techniques to Improve Performance

In the world of calisthenics, training effectiveness depends not only on physical strength or technique, but also on the ability to focus and manage one's breathing during exercise. Chapter 8, "Advanced Breathing and Concentration Techniques in Calisthenics," explores sophisticated methods for improving both breathing and concentration, two key components that can transform a workout from good to extraordinary.

This chapter is dedicated to providing athletes with the tools they need to make the most of every breath and every moment of focus. Through advanced breathing techniques, athletes can improve oxygenation, better manage energy and optimize recovery. In parallel, adopting meditation and visualization practices allows them to sharpen concentration, increase mental resilience and improve movement accuracy.

From breathing exercises that can be integrated during daily routines to meditation techniques that help maintain calm and focus under stress, this chapter offers a comprehensive guide for those seeking to elevate their performance in calisthenics through mental and physical control.

Through the regular adoption of these practices, calisthenics practitioners will discover how to transform not only their approach to training, but also their ability to face challenges and overcome obstacles, both in sports practice and in daily life.

Breathing control is one of the most underrated but essential techniques in improving athletic performance, especially in calisthenics. Breathing correctly during exercise can significantly increase the efficiency of each training session, improve endurance, and facilitate rapid recovery. In this chapter, we will explore how breathing affects athletic performance and how it can be optimized to improve concentration and physical performance.

Fundamentals of Breathing in Calisthenics: Breathing plays a crucial role in determining how effectively the body can perform during training and how it handles fatigue. During intense exercise, proper breathing ensures that adequate amounts of oxygen reach the muscles, which is essential for maintaining energy and strength. Shallow or inadequate breathing, on the other hand, can lead to rapid fatigue.

Breathing Techniques:

1. **Diaphragmatic Breathing**:
    - Also known as abdominal breathing, it is fundamental to effective training. It is practiced by breathing deeply through the nose, allowing the abdomen to fully expand, and then slowly exhaling through the mouth. This type of breathing increases oxygenation and improves endurance.

2. **Respiratory Rhythm During Exercise**:
    - Synchronizing breathing with movements can increase performance and prevent injury. For

example, inhaling during the downward phase of a squat and exhaling during the upward phase can help maintain adequate internal pressure in the body and support the movement.

3. **Rhythmic Breathing**:
   o Maintaining a regular breathing rhythm during repetitive exercises, such as push-ups or pull-ups, helps stabilize the core and maintain adequate energy distribution.

Benefits of Controlled Breathing:

- **Improved cardiovascular efficiency**:
   o Proper breathing not only supports muscle performance but also improves the efficiency of the cardiovascular system.

- **Reduction of stress and fatigue**:
   o Deep breathing has a calming effect on the nervous system, reducing stress and the perception of fatigue during training.

- **Improved pain control**:
   o The ability to manage breathing can help control the feeling of pain and discomfort during intense training sessions.

Integrating Breathing into the Calisthenics Routine: To effectively integrate breathing into your calisthenics routine, you should start with pre-workout breathing exercises to prepare your body and mind. In addition, breathing awareness should be maintained throughout the workout, paying attention to breathing patterns and adjusting them according to the intensity of the exercise.

Transitioning from breathing control to meditation, which will be explored in the next section 8.2, "Using Meditation to Improve Concentration," is another step in improving concentration and mental performance. This will not only refine physical skills but also sharpen the mind, which is essential for overcoming personal limitations and reaching new levels of performance.

8.2 Using Meditation to Improve Concentration

Meditation is a powerful tool that can significantly improve the focus and effectiveness of calisthenics training. Not only does this practice help reduce stress and anxiety, but it also improves the ability to focus, enabling athletes to perform complex movements with greater precision and control. In this chapter, we will explore different meditation techniques and how they can be integrated into the training routine to maximize mental and physical benefits.

Benefits of Meditation in Calisthenics:

- **Improved Focus**: Regular meditation helps develop the ability to focus on a single task, reducing distractions during exercise.

- **Stress Management**: By practicing meditation, one can learn to manage stress better, resulting in calmer and more controlled performance.

- **Better Recovery**: Meditation contributes to better mental and physical recovery, accelerating healing and decreasing recovery time.

- **Increased Body Awareness**: Meditative practice increases one's body awareness, which is essential for improving form and efficiency in performing exercises.

Types of Meditation for Athletes:

1. **Mindfulness Meditation:**
    - It focuses on living in the present moment without judgment. During mindfulness, one can meditate while sitting or while warming up, focusing on breathing or body sensations.
    - **Practice**: Dedicate 5-10 minutes before or after practice to sit quietly, close your eyes and focus your attention on the incoming and outgoing breath.

2. **Transcendental Meditation:**
    - Use a mantra, word or sound repeated silently to help focus the mind and transcend ordinary thinking.
    - **Practice**: Choose a mantra that is personal and meaningful and mentally repeat it in 20-minute sessions twice a day.

3. **Guided Visualization:**
    - It involves imagining positive and successful scenarios, improving motivation and self-efficacy.

- **Practice**: Visualize yourself as you successfully complete a calisthenics circuit, focusing on every movement and sensation.

Integrating Meditation into the Training Routine:

- **Daily Routine**: Begin and/or end each day with a short meditation session to stabilize pace and improve focus during workouts.
- **Before the Event**: Practice meditation on competition days or before particularly intense training sessions to reduce anxiety and increase concentration.
- **Active Recovery**: Incorporate meditation sessions on recovery days to promote deeper relaxation and mental recovery.

Overcoming the Challenges:

- **Consistency**: The key to benefiting from meditation is regular practice. Set daily reminders to keep the commitment.
- **Environment**: Find a quiet and comfortable place where you can meditate without interruption.

Meditation not only improves concentration but also the overall quality of life, making athletes more resilient both mentally and physically. This practice sets the stage for the next item, 8.3 "Visualization Techniques for Mental Preparation," where we will explore how to use visualization to mentally prepare for the challenges of calisthenics.

8.3 Visualization Techniques for Mental Preparation

Visualization is a powerful psychological technique that can significantly improve performance in calisthenics by allowing athletes to mentally practice skills before physically performing them. In this chapter, we will explore how visualization techniques can be used to prepare the mind and body for training challenges, thereby improving concentration and exercise effectiveness. This approach will be linked to the next section, 8.4 "Impact of Breathing on Post-Workout Recovery," to show how proper mental preparation can also positively influence recovery processes.

Fundamentals of Visualization: Visualization, or guided imagination, involves the act of creating clear and detailed mental images of yourself while perfectly performing an exercise. This method is based on the principle that the mind can be trained to induce desired physical reactions through simulated mental images.

Implementation of Visualization in Calisthenics:

1. **Definition of Visualization Objectives**:
    - Before starting, it is essential to clearly define what movements or results you want to visualize. This could include performing a specific number of pull-ups, completing a new movement such as a muscle-up, or simply maintaining proper form during a difficult exercise.

2. **Quiet Environment**:
    - Find a calm, distraction-free place where you can sit comfortably or lie down to practice

visualization. The absence of outside interruptions helps to maintain concentration on the mental images.

3. **Relaxation Techniques**:
    o Begin each visualization session with breathing or meditation techniques to relax the mind and body. This facilitates deeper immersion in mental imagery without tension or anxiety.

4. **Creating Vivid Images**:
    o Close your eyes and imagine yourself performing the exercise. Visualize every detail: the environment around you, the specific sounds of the workout, the feel of your moving muscles, and the intensity of the physical exertion. The more detailed the image, the more effective the visualization will be.

5. **Emotional Focus**:
    o Incorporate the emotions you anticipate feeling when you reach the goal. This can include feelings of success, strength, and joy. Positive emotion strengthens the connection between visualization and physical accomplishment of the exercises.

Regular Practice:
- Consistency is critical to success with visualization. Set aside time each day, ideally before or after workouts, to practice this technique. Even a few minutes a day can

make a big difference in your ability to perform mentally and physically.

Measuring Progress:

- Keep track of progress not only in physical terms but also in the ability to visualize clearly and maintain concentration for longer periods.

These visualization techniques not only mentally prepare the athlete to face and overcome physical challenges, but also improve the approach to training, making each session more intentional and focused. This mental preparation ties in closely with the next point, 8.4 "Impact of Breathing on Post-Workout Recovery," illustrating how a well-prepared mind can also positively influence physical recovery after activity.

8.4 Impact of Breathing on Post-Workout Recovery.

Breathing plays a crucial role not only during exercise but also in the post-workout recovery process. Proper breathing technique can accelerate muscle recovery, decrease fatigue, and improve the overall efficiency of the recovery process. In this chapter, we will examine how breathing affects recovery after training and how it can be optimized to maximize recovery benefits, linking this information to the next section 8.5 "Integrating Breathing and Meditation into the Daily Routine."

Fundamentals of Breathing for Recovery: After an intense calisthenics session, the body needs oxygen to help repair muscles and replenish energy stores. Deep, controlled breathing helps increase oxygen intake, thereby facilitating the removal of metabolic waste substances accumulated during the workout.

Breathing Techniques for Recovery:

1. **Diaphragmatic Breathing**:
   - This technique involves breathing deeply with the diaphragm rather than the chest muscles. It helps improve the effectiveness of oxygen flow in the lungs and blood, promoting faster recovery.
   - **Practice**: Lie on your back, put one hand on your abdomen and the other on your chest. Breathe deeply through your nose, making sure only your hand on your abdomen goes up.

2. **Breathing at 4-7-8**:
   - This technique helps calm the nervous system and reduce stress, which can be especially high after intense training.
   - **Practice**: Inhale counting to 4, hold your breath for 7 seconds, then exhale slowly counting to 8. Repeat for 4 cycles.

3. **Alternate Nostril Breathing**:
   - This technique from yoga helps balance the left and right sides of the brain, promoting relaxation and improving sleep quality, which is critical for effective recovery.
   - **Practice**: Sit with your back straight. Use the right thumb to close the right nostril, inhale from

the left, then close with the left index finger and exhale from the right. Continue alternating nostrils.

Benefits of Breathing in Recovery:

- **Decreased Heart Rate**: Deep breathing helps reduce heart rate, bringing the body into a calmer state and promoting recovery.

- **Improved Fatigue** Tolerance: Improving breathing efficiency increases the body's ability to tolerate fatigue, which is useful for future training sessions.

- **Reduction of Muscle Pain**: Deep breathing can also help reduce post-workout muscle pain through improving circulation and facilitating lactic acid elimination.

Integrating Breathing into Daily Recovery: Incorporate these breathing techniques as part of your cool-down routine. Devoting 5-10 minutes to guided breathing after training can greatly improve the recovery process.

These breathing practices should be integrated into a holistic approach that also includes meditation to get the most out of post-workout recovery. This brings us to the next section, 8.5 "Integrating Breathing and Meditation into the Daily Routine," where we will explore how to combine these breathing techniques with meditative practices for overall well-being and improved performance.

8.5 Integrating Breathing and Meditation into the Daily Routine

Integrating breathing and meditation techniques into daily routines not only improves physical performance but also contributes significantly to mental well-being. This chapter explores how to combine these practices to maximize their benefits, making them an essential part of daily life. This approach sets the stage for effectively overcoming mental barriers, as will be explored in more detail in the next section 9.1, "Identifying and Overcoming Mental Barriers."

Create a Daily Routine: To get the most benefit from breathing and meditation, it is important to establish a routine that fits easily into your lifestyle.

1. **Recommended Moments**:
   - **In the morning:** Start the day with 5-10 minutes of meditation and diaphragmatic breathing to center yourself and prepare yourself mentally and physically.
   - **Before training**: Use short breathing sessions to increase concentration and oxygenation, preparing the body for physical activity.
   - **After training**: Spend time relaxing and breathing to speed recovery and decrease cortisol, the stress hormone.
   - **Before bed**: Practice relaxing breathing or guided meditation to improve sleep quality.
2. **Integration into the work environment**:

- During breaks, perform short 1-2 minute breathing or meditation sessions to reduce stress and refresh the mind.

Effective Techniques for the Daily Routine: Regular adoption of specific techniques can make it easier to incorporate them into your daily life.

- **Breathing Techniques**:
  - **Breathing 4-7-8**: This is ideal for quick relaxation at any time of the day.
  - **Diaphragmatic breathing**: Use this technique throughout the day to maintain low levels of stress and anxiety.
- **Meditation**:
  - Mindfulness: Practice mindfulness during daily breaks, focusing on the present to quiet the mind.
  - **Walking meditation**: If possible, incorporate meditation while walking, even for short stretches, focusing on the rhythm of your steps and your breathing.

Benefits of Integrating Breathing and Meditation:

- **Improved Mental Health**: Reduced anxiety, improved concentration and increased serenity.
- **Improved Physical Performance**: Better body control, energy management, and increased efficiency in movements.

- **Faster** Recovery: Decreased recovery time between training sessions and improved pain tolerance.

Overcoming Integration Challenges:

- Consistency: The key to long-term benefit is consistent practice. Set reminders and alarms to help you maintain a routine.

- **Personalization**: Tailor the techniques to your lifestyle and personal preferences, choosing times and places that best suit your day.

In conclusion, the integration of breathing and meditation techniques not only prepares the body for physical activity but also fortifies the mind, making it more resilient to daily challenges. This mental preparation is essential to address and overcome psychological barriers in calisthenics, a topic that will be covered in the next chapter, "Identifying and Overcoming Mental Barriers."

Chapter 9: Overcoming Obstacles

9.1 Identify and overcome mental barriers

The journey in calisthenics, as in any discipline that requires commitment and dedication, is peppered with challenges and obstacles. Chapter 9, "Overcoming Obstacles," is dedicated to exploring and addressing the most common difficulties athletes encounter during their journey in calisthenics. This chapter offers concrete strategies and inspiration for overcoming physical, mental and emotional barriers that can hinder progress.

Through a series of insights and practical tips, readers will learn how to identify their personal barriers, whether physical limitations, mental blocks or drops in motivation. Techniques for strengthening resilience, improving perseverance and refining adaptability will be explored, essential elements for anyone wishing to excel in calisthenics.

From strategies for maintaining consistent motivation to methods for managing and overcoming pain and physical fatigue, this chapter equips athletes with the tools they need to advance despite adversity. In addition, approaches to turning obstacles into opportunities for growth and learning will be covered, emphasizing how each challenge overcome can become a stepping stone toward personal and athletic success.

"Overcoming Obstacles" is an essential chapter for all those who are ready to push their limits and turn challenges into triumphs, continuing with determination and focus in their calisthenics journey.

In calisthenics, as in any fitness journey, facing and overcoming mental barriers is critical to maintaining consistency and progress. Psychological challenges can undermine confidence, motivation, and lead to dropping out of workouts.

Fear of Not Being Good Enough: Many people fear not being up to the challenges of training, especially if they are beginners.

- **Causes**:
    - Comparisons with other people, images on social media, or negative past experiences can fuel this fear.
- **Strategies for Overcoming it**:
    - **Focus on Personal Progress**: Keep track of individual improvements, however small, to build confidence and maintain motivation.
    - **Accept Current Level**: Remember that everyone starts somewhere and that each skill level takes time and practice.

Sense of Guilt for Pauses: Guilt may arise when taking breaks from training or skipping scheduled sessions.

- **Causes**:
    - The pressure to stick to a rigid schedule or the fear of losing the progress made.
- **Strategies for Overcoming it**:

- **Flexibility**: Accept that breaks are necessary and beneficial to the body, providing time for recovery and injury prevention.
- **Realistic Scheduling**: Set a schedule that takes into account days off or unexpected schedule changes.

Fear of Failure: Fear of failing to achieve goals can lead to avoiding certain challenges or not giving one's all in training.

- **Causes**:
  - Overly high standards of perfectionism or a past experience of failure may reinforce this fear.
- **Strategies for Overcoming it**:
  - **Incremental Goals**: Set achievable short-term goals that can be successfully completed.
  - **Growth Mindset**: View mistakes as opportunities for learning and development.

Lack of Motivation: Motivation may decrease due to boredom or the feeling that efforts are not bringing tangible results.

- **Causes**:
  - Monotonous routines, unclear goals or lack of support can affect motivation.
- **Strategies for Overcoming it**:
  - **Variety in Workouts**: Introduce new challenges, exercises or change the order of the routine.

- **Social Support**: Training with a friend or joining a group can create a sense of mutual responsibility and motivation.
- **Recognize Progress**: Celebrate successes and recognize improvements even when they are minimal.

Workout Anxiety: Anxiety can result from insecurity about one's fitness or concern about potential injury.

- **Causes**:
  - Personal insecurity, previous physical trauma, or a lack of knowledge of proper techniques.
- **Strategies for Overcoming it**:
  - **Learn the Technique**: Take lessons or consult reliable resources to improve your understanding of the exercises.
  - **Practice Mindfulness**: Meditation or breathing exercises can help calm the mind.

In the next chapter, 9.2 "Managing Fatigue and Muscle Pain," we will discuss how to deal with physical fatigue and muscle pain to maintain the pace of training without compromising health and well-being.

9.2 Managing muscle fatigue and pain

Muscle fatigue and soreness are common effects of training, especially in calisthenics, where the body is constantly challenged. Although they are a natural part of the growth process, they must be managed properly to avoid overtraining or injury. In this chapter, we will examine strategies to manage muscle fatigue and soreness effectively, introducing the next section 9.3 "Recovery and Recovery Tips."

Understanding Fatigue: Fatigue can manifest as physical or mental exhaustion during or after training.

- **Causes**:
    - Too intense or frequent workouts without adequate rest days.
    - Inadequate diet, stress, lack of sleep, or underlying health problems.
- **Management**:
    - **Assess Intensity**: Make sure the training program is balanced, with intense training days alternating with light days.
    - **Nutrition**: Take nutritious meals that provide energy and aid muscle recovery.
    - **Hydration**: Staying hydrated is critical to support muscle function and prevent fatigue.

Understanding Muscle Pain: Muscle pain can be distinguished into exertional pain (DOMS) and injury pain.

- **Pain from Exertion (DOMS)**:
    - It typically appears 24-72 hours after training and indicates a process of muscle adaptation.
    - Caused by microinjuries in muscles during intense or novel exercises.

- **Injury pain**:
    - It is localized, persistent, and often manifests as swelling or limitation of movement.
    - It can be the result of incorrect technique or overtraining.

Muscle Pain Management: Taking preventive and recovery measures can help minimize muscle pain.

- **Warm-up and Defatigue**:
    - Proper warm-up prepares muscles for training, while defatigue reduces stiffness.
    - Devote at least 10-15 minutes to light movements, dynamic stretching and muscle activation.
- **Stretching and Mobility**:
    - Static stretching or foam rolling improves blood circulation and reduces muscle tension.
    - Joint mobility exercises help prevent stiffness and contractures.
- **Active Recovery**:
    - Light activities such as yoga, swimming or a walk promote circulation, accelerating muscle healing.
- **Relaxation Therapies**:

- Hot baths, massages and roller treatments can relieve tension and speed recovery.

Preventing Overtraining: Overtraining can have serious consequences for health and performance.

- **Signs of Overtraining**:
  - Decreased performance, irritability, sleep disturbances, and loss of motivation.
- **Prevention**:
  - **Rest Days**: Schedule at least one or two full rest days per week.
  - **Cycle Load**: Alternate cycles of intensive training with periods of light training.

In the next chapter, 9.3 "Recovery and Recovery Tips," we will explore in detail how to set up an effective recovery and recovery strategy to maintain optimal performance in calisthenics and ensure safe and consistent muscle growth.

9.3 Tips for recovery and recuperation

Recovery is an essential part of training, as important as the effort itself. It allows muscles to heal, grow and adapt to training stimuli, preventing overtraining and reducing the risk of injury. In this section, we will provide practical tips for optimizing recovery and recuperation, linking to the next section, 9.4 "Maintaining long-term motivation."

Rest and Sleep: Sleep is the fundamental pillar of recovery.

- **Duration**:

- Sleeping at least 7 to 9 hours per night ensures that the body has time to repair muscles and regenerate energy.

- **Quality**:
  - Creates a comfortable sleeping environment by maintaining a cool temperature and reducing light and noise sources.
  - Establish a pre-sleep routine, such as reading or light stretching, to relax and prepare your body for rest.

Active Recovery: Light physical activity promotes blood flow, accelerating recovery.

- **Light Exercises**:
  - Activities such as walking, swimming, or yoga promote the release of muscle tension.
- **Foam Rolling**:
  - Using a foam roller or massager can help release muscle tension and improve circulation.

Adequate Nutrition: Nutrition plays a critical role in recovery, providing nutrients for healing and muscle growth.

- **Protein**:
  - Consume high-quality protein (such as chicken, fish, legumes, and dairy products) within 30 to 60 minutes of training to facilitate protein synthesis.

- **Carbohydrates**:
    - Supplement complex carbohydrates (such as brown rice, sweet potatoes, and oats) to replenish glycogen stores.
- **Healthy Fats**:
    - Include unsaturated fats (such as avocado, olive oil, nuts, and seeds) to support hormone function and reduce inflammation.
- **Hydration**:
    - Stay hydrated by drinking water and supplementing electrolytes after intense workouts.

Stretching and Mobility: Stretching improves flexibility and reduces muscle stiffness.

- **Static Stretching**:
    - Hold each position for at least 20-30 seconds, focusing on the tense areas.
    - Avoid static stretching immediately before training, but it is ideal post-workout or as part of an evening routine.
- **Joint Mobility**:
    - Integrates joint mobility exercises to prevent stiffness and improve range of motion.

Massage and Therapies: Targeted treatments can relieve muscle tension and speed healing.

- **Massage**:
    - A sports or therapeutic massage can release muscle knots, improving circulation.
- **Cryotherapy and Thermotherapy**:
    - Alternating hot and cold baths or the use of ice packs can reduce inflammation and promote recovery.

Plan Rest Days: Including rest days in the training program is essential to prevent overtraining.

- **Active Rest**:
    - Integrate active rest days with light activities to maintain circulation without straining muscles.
- **Full Rest**:
    - Plan at least one full rest day per week for optimal recovery.

In the next chapter, 9.4 "Maintaining Long-Term Motivation," we will discuss strategies for maintaining motivation and enthusiasm toward training while addressing challenges that may arise during the fitness journey.

9.4 Maintaining long-term motivation

Maintaining long-term motivation is one of the biggest challenges when pursuing a fitness program. Even when the goals are clear and the routine is well structured, motivation can fluctuate over time. In this chapter, we will look at some effective strategies for maintaining motivation, introducing the next section 9.5 "How to manage plateaus."

Setting Meaningful Goals: Meaningful goals provide clear direction and a reason to keep pushing beyond daily challenges.

- **Short-Term Goals**:
  - Short-term goals, such as completing a new exercise or increasing repetitions, help generate quick and rewarding results.

- **Long-Term Goals**:
  - Goals such as entering a competition or reaching an advanced level in a particular exercise maintain focus over time.

Finding Social Support: Having the support of a training partner, coach or group can make the journey more engaging.

- **Responsibilities**:
  - A partner or coach can help you stay accountable for your progress by providing constructive feedback.

- **Shared Motivation**:
  - Training with friends or a group maintains interest and adds a social component to the program.

Variety in Workouts: Introducing novelty into routines helps prevent monotony.

- **Miscellaneous Exercises**:
  - Alternate exercises, incorporating new movements or variations to keep the workout fresh.
- **Alternative Activities**:
  - Try complementary activities such as rock climbing, swimming or team sports to challenge the body in new ways.

Celebrating Successes: Acknowledging achievements is essential to keeping morale high.

- **Small Victories**:
  - Celebrate small milestones, such as improving the number of repetitions or learning a new skill.
- **Significant Awards**:
  - For larger goals, plan a special reward such as a trip or a favorite activity.

Visualizing Success: Mental visualization is a powerful motivational tool.

- **Clear Image**:
  - Create a clear mental image of what you want to achieve, such as being able to perform muscle-ups or achieve a certain body composition.
- **Daily Visualization**:
  - Spend a few minutes each day visualizing yourself achieving your goals, solidifying this image in your mind.

Learning from Difficulties: Challenges and obstacles are part of the journey, but they can be used as opportunities for growth.

- **Resilience**:
  - Learn to see mistakes and failures as learning experiences to become stronger.
- **Adaptability**:
  - Be flexible in your approach and ready to change strategy when necessary.

Keeping a Journal: A personal journal can help you monitor progress and reflect on the journey.

- **Monitoring Progress**:
  - Document achievements, challenges overcome, and lessons learned.
- **Expression of Emotions**:
  - Use journaling to express thoughts and feelings, relieving stress and promoting a positive outlook.

In the next chapter, 9.5 "How to Handle Plateaus," we will discuss strategies for dealing with and overcoming plateaus, ensuring steady progress and minimizing frustration.

9.5 How to handle plateaus

Plateaus occur when progress stalls despite consistent efforts. They can be frustrating, but they are also a natural part of the training process and a challenge to overcome in order to continue to improve. In this section, we will discuss strategies for recognizing, understanding, and managing plateaus effectively, linking to the next section 10.1, "When you are ready for the intermediate level."

Understanding Plateaus: A plateau occurs when performance or physical improvement remains stagnant for an extended period.

- **Common causes**:
    - **Monotonous Routine**: Repetition of the same routine makes the body efficient in exercises, reducing the effectiveness of the workout.
    - **Overtraining**: Training without adequate rest can lead to chronic fatigue and an inability to improve.
    - **Lack of Progression**: Keeping the same intensity, load or number of repetitions prevents the body from receiving new stimuli.

Recognizing the Signs: Signs of a plateau can vary, but some common symptoms include:

- **Stagnation of the Force**:
    - Difficulty lifting heavier weights or increasing the number of repetitions.
- **Loss of Interest**:
    - Feeling of boredom or lack of motivation during training.

- **Fatigue**:
    - Persistent fatigue and longer recovery time.

Strategies for Overcoming Plateaus:

1. **Changing the Routine**:
    - **Varying Exercises**: Introduce new exercises or variations to challenge the body in different ways.
    - **New Order**: Change the order in which you perform exercises or the division of muscle groups.

2. **Adopting Progression**:
    - **Gradual Increments**: Increase weight or repetitions gradually to stimulate growth.
    - **Specific Progressions**: Introduce specific progressions for key exercises (such as one-arm push-ups to increase strength).

3. **Load Cycle**:
    - **Periodization**: Alternate periods of intensive training with lighter training cycles to allow the body to recover and adapt.

4. **Recovery and Rest**:
    - **Rest Days**: Be sure to include days of active rest and complete rest.
    - **Sleep and Nutrition**: Optimizes sleep and nutrition to support muscle healing and recovery.

5. **Diverse Goals**:

    - **New Challenges**: Set new goals or challenges to focus on a different area, such as improving cardio endurance or technical skill.
    - **Incremental Goals**: Set small interim goals to recognize progress and stay motivated.

Keeping a Journal: Documenting workouts and progress helps identify patterns that lead to plateauing.

- **Tracking Change**:
    - Note the changes made to the routine and compare them with the results obtained.
- **Identifying Trends**:
    - Look for patterns in performance to discover any external factors that might affect progress.

In the next chapter, 10.1 "When You're Ready for the Intermediate Level," we will discuss how to figure out when it is time to move to a more advanced routine and how to meet this new challenge to continue to grow in calisthenics.

Chapter 10: Going Beyond the Beginner

10.1 When you are ready for the intermediate level

Moving from beginner to intermediate level in calisthenics is an exciting time and a sign of significant progress. However, it is important to ensure that the body is prepared for the new challenges without risking injury. In this chapter, we will discuss the signs that indicate when you are ready to advance to the intermediate level and how to make the transition safely, linking to Section 10.2, "Introduction to More Complex Exercises," next.

Readiness Signals for the Intermediate Level: Transition to the intermediate level occurs when the body is sufficiently adapted to the basic exercises.

- **Strength and Endurance:**
    - You are able to comfortably perform a number of repetitions for key exercises without undue difficulty. For example:
        - **Push-ups**: 20 consecutive repetitions.
        - **Pull-ups**: 10 repetitions without assistance.
        - **Squat**: 30-40 repetitions.

- **Properly Executed Form**:
    - You can perform the key exercises with good form, without compromise.
- **Consistency**:
    - You exercise regularly at least 3-4 times a week without prolonged interruptions.
- **Recovery**:
    - You are able to recover adequately between training sessions.

Preparing for the Intermediate Level: Before advancing, it is important to make sure the body is ready for more complex challenges.

- **Mobility**:
    - Make sure joint mobility is adequate, especially for the shoulders, hips, and ankles.
- **Progressions**:
    - Integrates more challenging progressions to prepare the body for advanced exercises such as muscle-ups and pistol squats.
- **Nutrition**:
    - A proper diet becomes even more important to sustain energy and recovery.

Transition to More Complex Exercises: As you progress to the intermediate level, the exercises become more complex and require more control.

- **Add Weight:**
    - Introduce progressive overload, such as adding a belt with weights for pull-ups and dips.
- **Advanced Variants:**
    - Replace basic exercises with advanced variations:
        - **Push-ups**: One-arm push-ups, plyometric push-ups.
        - **Pull-ups**: Pull-ups with tighter grip, one-arm assisted pull-ups.
- **New Movements:**
    - Start learning more complex movements such as muscle-ups, handstand push-ups and pistol squats.

Programming the Intermediate Routine: The structure of the routine becomes more important at this level.

- **Circuit Training**:
    - Circuit workouts allow you to work multiple muscle groups in a single session, improving endurance and strength.
- **Breakdown of Muscle Groups**:
    - An effective division might be:
        - **Upper part**: pull-up, push-up, handstand.
        - **Lower part**: squats, lunges, pistol squats.

- **Gradual Progression**:
    - Do not go straight to extremely advanced exercises. Work on gradual progressions to master each new level.

Monitor Progress: Continuing to monitor progress is essential to avoid plateaus.

- **Periodic Testing**:
    - Evaluate the ability to increase the number of repetitions or load for each key exercise.
- **Record Progress**:
    - Keep a journal to note changes and make adjustments when necessary.

In the next chapter, 10.2 "Introduction to More Complex Exercises," we will discuss some of the more advanced techniques and movements that characterize the intermediate level and provide suggestions for mastering them.

10.2 Introduction to more complex exercises

Once you have reached the intermediate level in calisthenics, it is time to introduce more complex exercises that test strength, stability and coordination. These advanced exercises require precise technique and often require progressions to master. In this chapter, we will explore some of the more complex exercises and how to gradually integrate them into routines, linking to the next section 10.3, "Creating a supportive community."

Muscle-Up: The muscle-up combines pull-ups and dips, requiring explosive strength and coordination.

- **Progressions**:
    - **False Grip**: Start by learning the "false grip," a grip that allows you to make the transition.

    - **Explosive Pull-Up**: Perform explosive pull-ups to develop the strength needed to get over the bar.

- **Dip on Rings**: Strengthen the muscles involved in transition by performing dips on rings.
- **Final Exercise**:
  - Hold the bar firmly with the false grip, perform an explosive pull-up and quickly switch to the dip position.

Handstand: Handstand develops shoulder strength and core stability.

- **Progressions**:
  - **Wall Walks**: Start by walking your hands toward the wall until your body is upright.

  - **Handstand Wall**: Perform handstand by leaning your feet against the wall for support.
  - **Handstand Kick-Up**: Practice upward kicks until you reach the handstand position without a wall.

- **Final Exercise**:
    - Once you feel stable, try to keep your balance without support.

Pistol Squat: The pistol squat is a one-legged squat that improves balance, strength and mobility.

- **Progressions**:
    - **Box Pistol Squat**: Perform a pistol squat by sitting on a bench or box for ease of movement.
    - **Assisted**: Perform the pistol squat while holding a support to balance yourself.
    - **Negative**: Focus on controlled descent while maintaining balance.
- **Final Exercise**:
    - From standing, lift one leg in front of you and bend the other until you reach a squatting position, then return to standing.

Front Lever: The front lever is an isometric position that challenges core and upper body strength.

- **Progressions**:
    - **Tuck Front Lever**: Keep your knees bent toward your chest while keeping your body horizontal.

    - **Advanced Tuck**: Move your knees slightly away from your chest to increase the difficulty.
    - **One Leg Out**: Extend one leg while keeping the other bent.
- **Final Exercise**:
    - Extend both legs horizontally and keep your balance.

Planche: The planche is a free-body position that requires extreme strength and control.

- **Progressions:**
  - **Tuck Planche:** Keep knees bent close to chest and arms outstretched.

  - **Straddle Planche:** Open the legs in a spread position to reduce the difficulty.

  - **Band Planche:** Uses an elastic band to provide support during movement.
- **Final Exercise:**

- From a squatting position with your hands on the ground, extend your legs back until you reach a horizontal position.

In the next chapter, 10.3 "Creating a Supportive Community," we will discuss the importance of finding a group that can offer motivation and support as you work to master these complex exercises.

10.3 Creating a community of support

Calisthenics, like many fitness trails, can be improved through a supportive community. Finding or creating a group that shares the same goals and values can provide strong motivation, encouragement, and technical suggestions. In this section, we will discuss how to create a supportive community, linking to the next section 10.4 "Continuing Learning and Growth."

Benefits of a Support Community: Having a support group offers several benefits, both practical and emotional.

- **Motivation and Accountability**:
    - A group can help you stay accountable to your goals by encouraging you not to miss training sessions.
- **Knowledge Sharing**:
    - Other group members can offer technical suggestions and share strategies that have worked for them.
- **Sense of Belonging**:

- Belonging to a community with similar goals and challenges creates a sense of belonging and sharing.

Find an Existing Community: If there are groups in your area, it may be easier to join an already active community.

- **Calisthenics gyms or Park:**
  - Look for local gyms or dedicated parks where group training sessions are held.
- **Social Media**:
  - Find online groups on social media that organize workout meetings or share routines and tips.
- **Events and Competitions**:
  - Attend local competitions or calisthenics rallies to meet other enthusiasts and find a group that shares your interests.

Create Your Community: If no group exists in your area, consider starting your own.

- **Involve Friends**:
  - Invite friends or acquaintances who might be interested in calisthenics and encourage them to participate.
- **Organizing Regular Meetings**:
  - Schedule weekly or monthly meetings in an accessible place to train together.
- **Creating an Online Group**:

- Use social media platforms to create an online group where you can share updates, challenges and progress.

Group Activities: Engage the community with activities that motivate and keep them interested.

- **Circuit Training**:
  - Organize collective circuit training to encourage friendly competition.
- **Fitness Challenges**:
  - Create weekly or monthly challenges, such as who can do the most pull-ups or learn a new skill.
- **Technique Sessions**:
  - Invite more experienced members to lead technique or learning sessions to teach advanced exercises.

Emotional Support: Community is not only technical; it can offer valuable emotional support.

- **Mutual Encouragement**:
  - Encourage others to pursue their goals, recognizing and celebrating their progress.

- **Overcoming the Challenges**:
  - Be ready to listen and offer support when a group member faces a personal challenge or plateau.

Combine Training **and Socialization**: Combine the social aspect with training to make sessions more engaging.

- **Out-of-Training Activities**:
    - Organize social activities after training, such as lunch or a hike, to build deeper relationships.
- **Open Communication**:
    - Maintain open and regular communication with the group to better understand each person's needs and expectations.

In the next chapter, 10.4 "Continuing Learning and Growth," we will explore how to maintain a continuous growth approach, making the most of available resources to further improve in calisthenics.

10.4 Continuing learning and growth

Growth in calisthenics never stops. Even after reaching an advanced level, there is always something new to learn, experience, and master. Continuing to learn and grow ensures that the journey remains interesting, challenging, and enriching. In this chapter, we will look at how to maintain a continuous growth approach, linking to the next section 10.5, "Planning for the future of your fitness journey."

Learn New Skills: Exploring new movements and variations can keep motivation high and expand the repertoire of skills.

- **Handstand Walk and One-Arm Handstand**:

- Expand your skills with advanced handstand exercises, such as walking upright or performing a handstand on one arm.
- **Levers**:
- Master more difficult variations of front and back levers, working on progressions that add challenge.
- **Plyometric and Dynamic**:
  - Add plyometric and dynamic exercises, such as plyometric muscle-ups or clap push-ups, to improve power and explosiveness.

Attend Workshops and Courses: A coach or expert can provide new perspectives and teachings that enrich your routine.

- **Technical Workshops**:
  - Attend specific workshops to improve technique, form and progressions.
- **Online Courses**:
  - Find online courses from qualified instructors to learn new training methods and strategies.

Study Teaching Materials: Deepening your theoretical knowledge can help you better understand training principles.

- **Books and Articles**:
  - Read books and articles written by fitness experts to broaden your understanding of training methods.

- **Educational Videos**:
  - Watch educational videos of experienced athletes and coaches to discover new exercises or alternatives.

Experimenting with New Routines: Changing the structure of routines can offer new challenges and adaptations.

- **Alternative Circuits**:
  - Introduce alternative circuits that focus on different combinations of exercises.
- **Split Alternatives**:
  - Change the division of muscle groups, focusing on two main groups per session.

Getting Feedback: Receiving feedback from an outside source can help you improve form and identify blind spots.

- **Coach or Mentor**:
  - Work with a coach or mentor who can analyze your technique and offer detailed advice.
- **Training Partners**:
  - Ask your training partner to observe and report any mistakes or weaknesses.

Regularly Evaluate Progress: Evaluate progress periodically to identify areas for improvement and set new goals.

- **Fitness Testing**:
  - Perform regular fitness tests to monitor strength, endurance, and mobility.

- **Training Diary**:
    - Keep a detailed progress diary to analyze trends and improve training strategy.

Involve the Community: The community can be a valuable source of advice and inspiration.

- **Online Groups**:
    - Join online groups where enthusiasts share their experiences and routines.
- **Events and Competitions**:
    - Take part in local events or competitions to see new approaches and improve.

In the next chapter, 10.5 "Planning for the Future of Your Fitness Journey," we will look at how to set a clear and sustainable vision for the future of your calisthenics journey, ensuring continued growth and steady improvement.

10.5 Planning for the future of your fitness journey

After establishing a solid foundation in calisthenics, it is important to have a clear vision for the future of one's fitness journey. Effective planning ensures that progress is continuous and that training remains challenging and aligned with personal goals. In this final section of the book, we will explore strategies for planning for the future of one's path, integrating all the points covered so far.

Set New Goals: Goals provide clear direction and help maintain motivation.

- **Short Term**:

- Set achievable goals in the coming weeks or months, such as increasing the number of pull-ups or learning a new skill such as muscle-ups.
- **Long-Term**:
  - Set more ambitious goals that require time and dedication, such as entering a competition, performing advanced exercises such as the planche or completing a training course of a certain level.

Periodically Assess Progress: Monitoring progress ensures that current strategies are working and training is effective.

- **Periodic Testing**:
  - Plan periodic tests to assess strength, endurance, and technical skills, comparing results with previous performance.
- **Critical Analysis**:
  - Use the training diary to identify the most effective exercises and make changes where needed.

Adapt Routine to Goals: A routine must be flexible and adapt as your goals evolve.

- **Progression and Overload**:
  - Make sure the routine includes a gradual progression of loads or difficulties to stimulate growth.

- **Variations**:
  - Introduce variations in exercises to avoid monotony and address plateaus.

Balancing Workout with Lifestyle: Calisthenics must be sustainable and fit in with other personal and work commitments.

- **Planning Ahead**:
  - Create a weekly plan that takes into account the best times and days for training.
- **Managing Time**:
  - Integrates shorter but intense sessions during busy periods.

Maintaining Passion and Motivation: Finding ways to maintain passion helps keep you motivated.

- **Learning New Skills**:
  - Explore new skills such as front lever or flag to challenge yourself.
- **Involve Friends or Family**:
  - Working out with friends or family members makes training more fun and engaging.

Integrating Nutrition and Recovery: A comprehensive plan also takes nutrition and recovery into account.

- **Food Plan**:
  - Create an eating plan that supports fitness goals by providing the energy and protein needed to grow.

- **Recovery Strategies**:
    - Integrates rest days and activities such as yoga or foam rolling to prevent injury.

Maintain a Continuous Growth Approach: Learning never ends. Keep an open attitude to grow.

- **Resources**:
    - Continue to study books, articles, and videos that can improve your understanding of training.

- **Community**:
    - Stay active in the calisthenics community by sharing your experiences and learning from others.

Planning for the future of your fitness journey requires dedication, adaptability, and an ongoing commitment to growth. By following these principles, you will be able to continue to make progress and enjoy the benefits of a strong, flexible and resilient body through calisthenics.

If you think you liked this book and it helped you, I only ask you to take a few seconds to leave a short review on Amazon!

Thank you,

Francesco Martini